Strategic Studies Institute
and
U.S. Army War College Press

DEMOCRATIZATION AND INSTABILITY IN UKRAINE, GEORGIA, AND BELARUS

Robert Nalbandov

June 2014

*****

Comments pertaining to this report are invited and should be forwarded to: Director, Strategic Studies Institute and U.S. Army War College Press, U.S. Army War College, 47 Ashburn Drive, Carlisle, PA 17013-5010.

*****

This manuscript was funded by the U.S. Army War College External Research Associates Program. Information on this program is available on our website, *www.StrategicStudies Institute.army.mil*, at the Opportunities tab.

*****

*****

The Strategic Studies Institute and U.S. Army War College Press publishes a monthly email newsletter to update the national security community on the research of our analysts, recent and forthcoming publications, and upcoming conferences sponsored by the Institute. Each newsletter also provides a strategic commentary by one of our research analysts. If you are interested in receiving this newsletter, please subscribe on the SSI website at *www.StrategicStudiesInstitute.army.mil/newsletter*.

******

I would like to extend my sincere appreciate to the Strategic Studies Institute for supporting this project. My research on the role of political culture in institutional transformations in post-imperial and post-colonial societies will continue to grow. I would like to especially thank Dr. Korneli Kakachia, Associate Professor, Tbilisi State University; Roland Kovacs, Country Director in Ukraine, Pact, Inc.; Hanna Shelest, Senior Researcher at National Institute for Strategic Studies, Ukraine; Sergiy Shtukarin, Executive Director at Center for Political Studies, Ukraine; and numerous content experts from Belarus. I am greatly indebted to the organizers of the "6th Kyiv Security Forum 'Security In An Unsecure World'" which I had the pleasure of attending.

FOREWORD

Nations democratize at a different pace: Some achieve high governance standards, lasting political stability, and robust economies; others are lingering in their desires to look and act like their democratic counterparts. While no country strictly follows similar patterns of democratic institutionalization, there is a variable that defines the rate of success of their efforts: their political culture.

The empirical study by Dr. Robert Nalbandov unveils this "democratization puzzle" of incongruence between the levels of democracy, internal peace, and economic prosperity between the newly independent states of Ukraine, Georgia, and Belarus. By investigating the political cultures of the three post-Soviet countries, Dr. Nalbandov concludes that it was the distinct political cultures of these states (flexible in Georgia, rigid in Belarus, and bifurcate in Ukraine) that produced diverse outcomes in each specific case.

The Strategic Studies Institute is pleased to offer this monograph, which gives valuable insights into the matters of democratization in politically volatile new environments. The three patterns of political cultures identified in the monograph can be easily generalized and applied in most instances of new nation-building projects. The recommendations for the U.S. military and the government produced by the analysis provide the roadmap for short- and long-term partnerships in the countries of post-Soviet space.

DOUGLAS C. LOVELACE, JR.
Director
Strategic Studies Institute and
    U.S. Army War College Press

ABOUT THE AUTHOR

ROBERT NALBANDOV is currently an Assistant Professor of Political Science at the Utah State University where he teaches the courses on U.S. foreign policy and European and Russian politics and security. Since 2008, he has taught at Macalester College, St. Paul, Minnesota; University of St. Andrews, Scotland; University of Birmingham, England; Smolny College of Liberal Arts, St. Petersburg University, Russia; and Center for Security Studies, Angelo State University, Texas. Dr. Nalbandov is the author of *Foreign Interventions in Ethnic Conflicts* (Ashgate Publishing, 2009) and numerous articles on international and regional security, counterterrorism and U.S. foreign policy. He is currently working on his new book entitled *Russia's New Foreign Policy* (University of Nebraska Press, forthcoming). Dr. Nalbandov holds a Ph.D. in political science from the Central European University, Budapest, Hungary.

SUMMARY

This manuscript analyzes the interconnections between the democratic institutionalization of the newly independent states using the examples of Ukraine, Georgia, and Belarus, their political (in)stability, and economic development and prosperity. By introducing the concept of **regime mimicry** into the field of public administration, the author expands the epistemological frameworks of the democratization school to the phenomenon of **political culture**. Successes and failures of the democratic institutionalization processes in these countries largely depend on the ways their institutional actors reacted to internal and external disturbances of their domestic political, economic, and cultural environments. While Georgia's political culture revealed the highest degree of flexibility in accepting the externally proposed institutional frameworks and practices, the bifurcate political culture in Ukraine impeded its democratic institutionalization, while the rigid political culture in Belarus completely stalled the process of institutional transformations.

DEMOCRATIZATION AND INSTABILITY IN UKRAINE, GEORGIA, AND BELARUS

INTRODUCTION

In 1991, the process of liberalization of political, economic, and cultural settings in the post-Soviet countries came somewhat unexpectedly to many. After 70 years of existence under communist rule, and notwithstanding the wide cultural diversity of the former Soviet republics, all of them decided to take a path toward democratization, at least nominally. Out of the political systems previously tested elsewhere, all the former Soviet republics settled on democracy, which was considered the best choice possible. With the assistance of the Western democratic world, the newly established, but historically well-placed, nations were rapidly exposed to the democratic realities of politics, economy, and culture existing elsewhere in the form of democratic institutions. The choice for a democratic way seemed obvious: What was working "out there" should work here, too. Democratization enjoyed the overwhelming consensus among the newly independent states, not only as the evolutionary hallmark among the existing and empirically tested governance regimes, but also as the preferred choice for the newly created nation-states across the geographic regions.

While the ex-Soviet republics had the same starting point in their newly independent existence (the end of Soviet rule), three countries—Georgia, Ukraine, and Belarus—in particular stand out with regard to the diverse outcomes of their democratization processes. Moving away from the Soviet Union was difficult, and the choice of democratic governance was, in a way, the hardest transformation the three countries had

1

ever faced in their histories. The results in each of the three cases show a remarkable diversity. Georgia became the champion of public administration and economic reforms, turning it from the hotbed of Soviet corruption into the "beacon of democracy." Belarus has been suffering for 2 decades from the authoritarian governance of its lifelong president, Alexander Lukashenka. Finally, Ukraine occupies somewhat of a middle ground with its half-stagnant democratization after the disillusionment from the Orange Revolution of 2005.

Democracy — with the institutions of rule of law, free market relations, the spirit of equality, and protection of human rights and fundamental freedoms — is popularly considered the most conducive regime for building political stability and economic and social development. From an institutional standpoint, democracy, as the process of creation and interaction of the "socially shared rules, usually unwritten, that are created, communicated, and enforced outside officially" by the domestic policy (the citizenry) as well as "through channels that are widely accepted as official,"[1] involves the synergy of formal institutions (free courts, transparent elections, three branches of power, ombudsmen's office, etc.) as well as informal ones (rule of law, human rights).

From the point of political stability and economic and social development, democracy, according to Yi Feng:

> tends to have a positive effect on economic growth by inhibiting extra-constitutional political change and favouring constitutional political change. Democracy provides a stable political environment, which reduces unconstitutional government change at the macro level; yet along with regime stability, democracy of-

fers flexibility and the opportunity for substantial political change within the political system.[2]

The reality in Georgia, Belarus, and Ukraine, however, proves different. The impact of democracy on these variables is quite diverse in the three countries in focus. Georgia, the most democratically advanced state, has had the worst performance concerning its domestic political stability. The authoritarian rule in Belarus is the clear case of a nondemocratic society, which is, surprisingly, better developed economically and quite stable politically than the other two countries. The situation in Ukraine displays a weak correlation between the democratization level, on the one hand, and political stability and economic prosperity on the other.

The issue of political stability under the rapidly democratizing and volatile domestic environments is of utmost importance. Diverse outcomes of post-communist liberalization efforts under similar starting points represent the **governance puzzle** for the democratization literature. The puzzle raises a number of questions on the reasons for and durability of the democratization process. What makes democracy such an appealing regime for post-authoritarian and post-colonial societies to follow? How stable is the process of democratic nation-building after the initial installation of the institutions of democratic governance? Finally, can the future of political stability in the target countries be predicted given their current level of democratization and economic development?

The governance puzzle rests upon a number of premises. First, it assumes the existence of causal linkages between the level of democracy and overall political stability. It is popularly viewed that the more advanced the democracy, the lower the level of internal and external political disturbances. In general, democracy is positively related to overall stability. According to Feng:

> democracy will increase the probability of major regular government change, lessen the chances of irregular government change, and, in the long run, decrease the propensity for minor regular government change.[3]

Democracies, therefore, are more conducive to peaceful and systematic political change than violent sporadic transformations in their autocratic counterparts.

The second part of the governance puzzle is hidden in the variables that influence the level of democratization and, in turn, are influenced by the latter. The first such variable is economic development. There is a commonly accepted view that more prosperous countries tend to be more democratic than their poorer counterparts. According to K. Lundell:

> when countries become more affluent, the prospects of democracy increase. Countries with a high level of socio-economic development tend to be democratic, whereas poor countries most often lack democratic institutions and procedures.[4]

Susanna Lundström believes:

> the effect of democracy on economic freedom is positive and robust, supporting the so-called compatibility view . . . [A] higher level of democracy leads to an increased reliance on the market as the allocation mechanism, and to decreased restraints on international trade.[5]

4

Internally, democracy is considered to offer a larger degree and variety of freedoms than any other governance regime, including the protection of the economic and political rights. It creates incentives via reasonable taxes and free and fair economic legislation for the increased turnover of goods, services, and money, thus cutting the costs of economic transactions. It also protects businesses from unbridled tyranny of bureaucrats, corrupt officials, and life-threatening environments, allowing for them to operate and flourish.

The second variable is the third party participation, which can be critical domestic political landscapes of the target countries. This influence can be both aggravating and mitigating the forces existing on the domestic levels. External players may directly contribute to the economies and finances of their protégés and act as "external homelands"[6] for the ethnic groups residing within the borders of states in question, their "surrogate lobby-states"[7] without ethnic linkages, or intervene out of personal reasons in the existing rivalry between the political groups by skewing the local power balance towards the parties they support.[8] Third parties thus can have a very important role in redirecting the course of the democratization events depending on their own views with regards to the target countries and the domestic situation per se.

Finally, diverse political cultures of the nations are the very meta-variable influencing the outcomes of the democratization processes from the point of their acceptance, endurance, or rejection by the target societies. Political cultures bring the identity components into the democratic institutionalization equation. On a domestic level, they define the modes of interactions within various actors of the domestic institutional actors and their reactions on the internal political processes. On a broader scale, political cultures presuppose responses of the local polity to the external challenges and disturbances. Overall, political cultures are the necessary ingredients for defining the longevity of the governance regimes, in general, and individual rulers, in particular.

The empirical evidence from Georgia, Ukraine, and Belarus reveals a very interesting deviation of the commonly accepted patterns. Diversity between the levels of democratization, political stability, and economic development in Georgia, Ukraine, and Belarus can be explained by two factors. The first explanation of political stability in the countries with low democracy indicators is their "authoritarian resilience."[9] Autocratic regimes are usually more successful in stifling their opposition forces than democracies. On the one hand, it is the low degree of freedom and disregard for general human rights that the "autocracies" enjoy. The other reason for the political longevity and domestic stability of the autocracies is their strict control over their own public administration apparatus. The vertical hierarchy of governance allows authoritarian leaders to suppress public processes and keeps all the reins of power in their hands. The other side of the "governance puzzle" is the fact that countries with high levels of democratization, such as Georgia, have low levels of political stability. This phenomenon can be explained by the highly volatile domestic environment and presence of interest groups, which do not abide by the common rules of political engagement.

The connection between the levels of democracy and economic and social development in the three countries also seems to refute the ascribed power of democratic governance. The example of Georgia as having the lowest economic and social development indicators, as opposed to Belarus, which is on the other end of the developmental spectrum, shows that seemingly causal links between these two variables mostly belong to the theoretical field. Even in autocracies, there can be well-established and affluent middle and upper-middle classes that are more interested in keeping their wealth than in political freedoms. Likewise, hectic political domains prevent proper economic development and hinder social progress between the institutional actors: citizens, their organized societal groups, nongovernmental organizations (NGOs), mass media, and the institutions of governance.

In order to test the governance puzzle and see whether democracy plays the assumed important role in the matter of political stability and socio-economic development, two working hypotheses will be tested. The first one, the null hypothesis, postulates a reverse relation between democracy as the independent variable and political stability as the dependent variable. According to such a pessimistic vision, in newly democratizing societies, democracy is unable to prevent internal disturbances and external pressure or foster economic development. The second hypothesis engages in deeper exploration of the "democracy-stability-development" nexus by bringing in two intervening variables—economic development and political culture—and viewing them as being influenced by the factors of "authoritarian resilience" and "third-party interest"—to examine political stability from internal and external perspectives.

The authoritarian resilience of the ruling elite, which manages to coerce successfully the domestic institutional actors and to dissuade them from seeking political freedoms, presents the internal side of political stability. The assumption behind this factor postulates that, in the absence of authoritarian resilience, countries with unstable political cultures tend to display higher levels of political volatility and unrelenting rivalry between domestic institutional actors. The second variable investigates the external side of political stability by bringing in third-party factors. The assumption of this variable is that external actors can support/hinder the domestic political stability of the target countries by contributing to or decreasing the durability of the existing governance regimes, and providing for or lessening the financial well-being of their populations. The ultimate and much broader issue here is whether it is possible to credibly predict the internal political developments in newly established nations based on the examples of these three post-Soviet countries.

DEMOCRATIZATION/POLITICAL STABILITY/ SOCIAL DEVELOPMENT

Among all the governance regimes, democracies enjoy the closest synergy of efficiency and legitimacy because they offer the widest possible mechanisms for public participation in the evaluation of these qualities. Political stability, one of the main tasks of any governance regime, is widely viewed as:

> the capacity of a country to withstand internal and external shocks or crises.[10] Internally, stability is created by "members of society restrict[ing] themselves to the behavior patterns that fall within the limits imposed by political role expectations. Any act that deviates from these limits is an instance of political instability.[11]

Internal political stability embraces the wide array of interactions between institutional actors. Internal political stability keeps countries' integrity and prevents them from falling apart under the weight of domestic disturbances. External stability helps them resist economic, political, or military pressure from abroad. If chronic and unresolved, internal instability can lead to the failure of governments to satisfy the basic needs of their populations, which will eventually lead to their failure. Such failed states, or "cadaverous states," as Ahmed Samatar calls them,[12] with practically no civil life, no "central, regional, or local administrations . . . [no] public utility services, no electricity, no communications, no health services, [and] no schools,"[13] have no visible prospects for peace. From this point of view, political stability means "the degree to which political institutions are sufficiently stable to support the needs of [their] citizens, businesses, and overseas investors,"[14] as defined by the *Global Peace Index*.

Ideally, internal stability should mean peaceful responses to institutionalized succession of powers via the planned long-term and peaceful change of political leadership through constitutional means without resorting to violence and adjustment policies. In its most developed form, it is the ability of a political system to ensure the functioning of its institutional structures of power (the interaction of the branches of government and their agencies), as defined in the constitution of the political model. In this ideal model, conflicts among the actors are resolved within the countries' constitutions and are not accompanied by the revision of powers of political institutions on the basis of illegal factors, such as the dictate of a political leader, the use of direct force of pressure, or threat of illegitimate use of force. Externally, such a model would prevent any foreign control over domestic affairs, including direct management from abroad or indirect interventions. This essentially means the absence of any significant influence of extra-systemic political agents that can dramatically change the political landscape in the country.

Democracy and Political Stability.

For governance regimes to be successful and sustainable with regards to internal and external political stability and economic and social development, two qualities are necessary, according to Seymour Martin Lipset: effectiveness and legitimacy. By effectiveness, Lipset means:

> the actual performance of a political system, the extent to which it satisfies the basic function of government as defined by the expectations of most of members of a society, and the expectations of powerful groups within it which might threaten the system. . . .[15]

Legitimacy in this context is the "capacity of a political system to engender and maintain the belief that existing political institutions are the most appropriate or proper ones for the society."[16] Jack Goldstone capitalizes on Lipset's model and argues:

> Effectiveness reflects how well the state carries out state functions such as providing security, promoting economic growth, making law and policy, and delivering social services. Legitimacy reflects whether state actions are perceived by elites and the population as 'just' or 'reasonable' in terms of prevailing social norms.[17]

The combined legitimacy and effectiveness of governance is a prerequisite for political stability in most societies, regardless of their governance regimes. The difference is in the sources of internal and external stability. In democratic societies, internal political stability is based on "the rule of law, strong institutions rather than powerful individuals, a responsive and efficient bureaucracy, low corruption, and a business climate that is conducive to investment."[18]

These democratic institutions serve a dual purpose: They cut the transaction costs for its actors (citizens) and, at the same time, limit the options available for them. The first task is achieved by offering greater opportunities for self-expression and active participation in the decisions vital for their communities and countries. Citizens would have fewer reasons to revolt against their governments if they felt they received due protection concerning law and order. The effectiveness of democratic governance spreads over the majority of the institutional actors; legitimacy is created via the free and fair expression of their choice. Fulfillment of the second task is more complicated. Feng assumes that the more developed the democracy, the lower the level of internal political disturbances, thus:

> democracy will increase the probability of major regular government change, lessen the chances of irregular government change, and, in the long run, decrease the propensity for minor regular government change.[19]

This means that the institutional arrangements in place limit the changes for sporadic political activity while increasing the steady flows of political processes based on effective dialogues between governments and their citizens.

External political stability is created through peaceful interactions between the governments in question and foreign actors. Unstable countries attract parochial interests of their immediate and distant neighboring states that are trying to capitalize on inefficient governance, internal violence, and low levels of law and order. Paul Collier holds that the lack of internal stability imposes significant costs on the regional stability because the "neighbourhood spill-overs give the foreign actors 'reasonable claim to the right of intervention in order to reduce them'."[20] External political stability is also desirable "because it provides external players with the advantage of dealing with a government whose actions are predictable,"[21] which contributes to the political, economic, and social developments of the nations in question.

Durability of internal and external political stability is closely related to the notion of a "social contract." First appearing in the trial of Socrates,[22] "social contract" is a mode of citizen/government interaction, essentially between the citizens themselves and the government, which acts as an external arbiter and guardian of domestic stability. In this line of reasoning, John Locke views the political power as:

> a right of making laws with penalties of death, and consequently all less penalties, for the regulating and preserving of property, and of employing the force of the community, in the execution of such laws, and in the defence of the common-wealth from foreign injury; and all this only for the public good.[23]

An interesting aspect of any social contract is that it can exist under both autocratic and democratic regimes. The difference between the democratic and authoritarian social contract is its durability and the fulfillment of the "public good" obligation of the governments.

Longevity of the social contract ultimately defines the durability of the governance regime. This view on stability fulfills Lipset's requirement for the legitimacy of state, where "groups will regard a political system as legitimate or illegitimate according to the way in which its values fit in with their primary values,"[24] and Aaron Wildavski's political socialization, where "shared values [are] legitimating social practices."[25] These views on political stability include both prerequisites: internal (the societal "fit" and legitimacy) and external (the recognition of the international community). Problems in providing these prerequisites by the governments are referred to, by Charles Call, as the "internal" and "external" legitimacy gaps "where a significant portion of its political elites and society reject the rules regulating the exercise of power and the accumulation and distribution of wealth" and "when other states fail to recognize or accept its borders or its internal regime,"[26] respectively.

Historically, political stability depended on the will of the ruling autocrat. Under the monarchic autocratic rule of medieval Europe, people were deprived of security, rendering their everyday lives extremely unstable. In the jungle of human interactions populated by "solitary, poore, nasty, brutish" men, the Law of Nature dictated the "warre of every men against every men."[27] Internal political stability in monarchies rested upon the fear of their subjects for their lives in the omnipresent anarchy and uncertainty of the realities and their trust of the benevolence of the rulers who governed upon their sole discretion without any notion of public accountability. Similar to as it was in medieval Europe, social contract is also present in modern autocracies around the globe, but there, according to Vital Silitski, it:

> is asymmetrical in its nature. . . . [T]he state proposes the social contract in order to nip public discontent in the bud, without resorting to excessive punitive actions. . . . The asymmetrical nature of the social contract is caused by the inability of social groups to self-organize and elaborate horizontal contractual agreements.[28]

The key variable that differentiates democratic social contract from the autocratic one is the source of power. Whereas in democracies the power vested upon governments comes from their subjects, in autocracies:

> it is the state, and not civil society, that sets the framework of the consensus by offering material and non-material benefits in exchange for citizens' loyalty.[29]

Autocracies have different paths to political stability through the social contracts. The durability of those contracts is achieved by their "authoritarian resilience,"[30] i.e., the tenaciousness of leaders to stay in power by providing for the basic needs of most of their subjects and effective mechanisms of coercion. In most cases, the authoritarian resilience is based on two pillars: coercion of the population and providing them with limited benefits. The fruits of the effectiveness of governance are offered to limited groups of elite individuals (usually power actors and oligarchs) closely affiliated with the ruling autocrats, creating the unique rational choice-based societal "fit": the more benefits these groups receive from the governance, the "fitter" and more legitimate would be the regime.

Similar to democracies, autocracies provide benefits to the rest of the population; however, while in democracy:

> citizens both decide the size of government and have a right to the fiscal residuum, [in] autocracy . . . the state apparatus both decides the size of government and can appropriate the fiscal residuum.[31]

Due to the limits established by autocracies on civil participation in the political and economic lives of their countries, the benefits are provided to a much narrower extent. Autocracies aim at satisfying the basic needs of larger populations while keeping the better and, ultimately, lavish lifestyles of the "close circles," allowing them to enjoy disproportionally larger benefits. That is why the middle-class layers in these societies are extremely thin. The individuals from the privileged groups, on the other hand, enjoy free and flexible interpretation of both the letter and the spirit of the law, including economic legislation, and receive preferential treatment by the institutions of governance—all of which falls under the umbrella of "corruption."

The societal "fit" within the groups deprived of the benefits depends entirely on the effectiveness of coercion. The stronger the punitive mechanism of governance, in other words, the more "resilient" the regime is, the "fitter" it feels within the society. Autocracies use the government apparatus, commonly referred to in post-Soviet societies as "the administrative resources," to limit the freedoms of their citizens and to disregard general human rights. Use of law and order as punitive mechanisms coerces subjects to the point where any expression of free will is punitive by definition. In comparison, durability of the social contracts for democracies depends on the constant dialogue between the government and the electorate, which is accomplished through wide civil participation in the institutional frameworks offered by democracies. Kant considered republican governance, i.e., government elected by people, as the most viable basis for building long-lasting peaceful relations within and between nations. He believed that what makes democracy unique is that:

> First, it accords with the principles of **freedom** of the members of a society (as men), second, it accords with the principles of **dependence** of everyone on a single common [source of legislation] (as subjects), and, third, it accords with the law of the equality of them all (as citizens) [emphasis provided].[32]

Effective fulfillment of the Kantian trinity leads to the "republican government," or democracy, which decreases structural conflicts within societies and among them based on people's conscious decisions to prosper rather than conflict.

In modern times, Kantian ideas were further elaborated by John R. Oneal. and Bruce Russett to fill the requirements of modern political realities. The "Democratic Peace Theory,"[33] heavily based on Kantian views of republican constitutions, economic freedoms, and world governance, used a three-prong approach to political stability: democratically elected governments; increased role of intergovernmental organizations (IGOs), such as institutions offering nonconflictual means of communications between the states; and the complex economic interdependence that ties the countries together in the mutually beneficial knots of trade and fiscal exchange. The result of the interplay of these factors is that democracies are positively correlated with political stability since the two democracies would rather cooperate than fight.

Democracy is an evolutionary better suitable form for achieving domestic and international political stability on the basis of Kantian arrangements developed by citizens and vested upon their governments. In democracies, social contracts are concluded between the people and safeguarded by their elected governments, who are held constantly accountable to their electorate for proper fulfillment of the terms of the contract, i.e., their election promises. Politics in democracies also depend on the "resilience" of the regime, but in this case, the resilience is "democratic," based on the willingness and ability of its citizens to participate in the political processes and, similar to autocracies, the benefits offered to them by their democratically elected government. Coercion is, by definition, absent in democratic resilience and the effectiveness of the regime is nondiscriminatory.

Democracy and Economic Development.

A very significant aspect of the democratic governance is its link with economic development and prosperity and, ultimately, peace. This link has been enshrined in Preliminary Article 4 of the Kantian Perpetual Peace as one of the preconditions for peaceful relations among the nations on the international arena: "National debts shall not be contracted with a view to the external friction of states."[34] However, what might be obvious, at first—that democracy is good for economic development—would appear to be a much more complicated interaction, if closely examined. Democracy may, indeed, be considered to have a positive effect on economic development, a significant part of which is the respect for individual property rights and free market relations. The major assumption in political economic literature is that democracies, with their strong power actors in the form of businesses free from state control and independent trade units, are closely related to Smithsonian *"laissez faire"*[35] approaches, whereas autocracies, with their strict control over monetary flows and investments via referential elitist politics, are more restrictive in market relations.

The connection between democracy and economic development is double-sided. On the one hand, it is commonly assumed that:

> the more well-to-do a nation, the greater the chances that it will sustain democracy . . . [O]nly in a wealthy society in which relatively few citizens lived in real poverty could a situation exist in which the mass of the population could intelligently participate in politics and could develop the self-restraint necessary to avoid succumbing to the appeals of irresponsible demagogies.[36]

Krister Lundell also supports the idea of democracy being conducive to economic development:

> When countries become more affluent, the prospects of democracy increase. Countries with a high level of socio-economic development tend to be democratic, whereas poor countries most often lack democratic institutions and procedures.[37]

The middle classes represent the sources for support for democracies because the latter provide the benefits for the considerably wider circles of stakeholders than the autocracies. Societies that can afford wealthy middle classes are, thus, more inclined to uphold the social contracts with their democratically elected governments than autocracies since they have more assets to lose than the oppressed lower-income societies, e.g., free market relations and self-expression.

The opposite interpretation of the nature of the link between democracy and economic development is that the former promotes the latter. Milton Friedman argues that the more democratic the societies are, the more political and economic rights they offer to their populations.[38] According to Feng, democracies, together with:

> the existence and exercise of fundamental civil liberties and political rights, generate the social conditions most conducive to economic development. Political and economic freedom enhances property rights and market competition, thus promoting economic growth.[39]

Democratically elected governments are more accountable to their citizenry than autocracies, which are based on unchecked, unrestrained, and uncontrolled powers of the absolutist regimes. Citizens can use impartial and transparent democratic institutions, such as courts and law and order agencies, to obtain support for their economic activities and to seek remedies in case of violation of their rights, including economic rights. Under the autocracies, these institutions resembling their democratic counterparts may exist as well, but they would have only nominal roles. The real interaction between governments and citizens in autocracies happens via other institutional mechanisms, for example, institutionalized corruption. The citizens enjoy selective rights and receive preferential treatment depending on the distance to the ruling elites: the closer they are with those in power, the more they benefit from freedoms, including economic freedoms.

Yet the third, somewhat counterintuitive, view is that democracy is detrimental for economic development. Here, again, market arrangements and property rights come into play. As Adam Przeworski and Fernando Limongi note:

> The main mechanisms by which democracy is thought to hinder growth are pressures for immediate consumption, which reduce investment. Only states that are institutionally insulated from such pressures can resist them, and democratic states are not.[40]

Democracy facilitates consumerist society, which craves for exceedingly more wealth than is available at the expense of capital investments. The same authors conclude:

> [D]emocracy generates an explosion of demands for current consumption. These demands, in turn, threaten profits; hence, they reduce investment and retard growth. Democracy is thus inimical to economic development.[41]

In *laissez faire* societies where the governments have little, if any, control over market relations, fiscal bubbles are frequent. Crises of financial overextension and fiscal overexpansion lead to unchecked and uncontrolled information provided to the market actors.

The statistic analysis of Edward Mansfield *et al.* explains this phenomenon of the separation of the branches of government and the checks and balances existing between them. According to their research:

Having a legislature that ratifies the chief executive's trade proposals may create a credible threat that allows executives in democracies to arrive at freer trade outcomes than would otherwise occur. The possible veto of a trade deal by one or both legislatures in the dyad may lead the executives to search for lower mutually acceptable levels of trade barriers. This, in turn, may explain why pairs of democracies are better able to lower their trade barriers than mixed pairs.[42]

In this view, too much openness of democracies to the globalization processes and their overdependence on each other lead to the negative domino effects.

Autocracies, on the other hand, tend to trade with a limited number of like-minded states, hence the low potential of global financial disturbances caused by them. Together with the limited trade and economic privileges of minority societal groups, autocracies, paradoxically, can bring economic growth. According to Przeworski and Limongi, "'[S]tate autonomy' favors growth, and 'state autonomy' is possible only under authoritarianism."[43] The main idea here is that the notion of state autonomy positively correlates with performance of domestic economies. This is the opposite side of *laissez-faire*, a sort of Keynesian vision on economy[44] as influenced by governance regimes. The more the government is involved in regulating market relations, the more it is able to prevent situations similar to fiscal bubbles from happening by its regulatory actions. A typical institutional example of the "command-and-control" economy was the Ministry of Foreign Trade of the Union of Soviet Socialist Republics (USSR), the only body representing Soviet industries in external interactions. Such governing from above is, obviously, negative from the point of view of limiting the freedoms of the market actors but, at the same time, a command-and-control economy provides protection to the businesses in case of negative external influences.

DEMOCRATIZATION IN NUMBERS

Interplay between the variables of democratization, political stability, and economic and social development in Ukraine, Georgia, and Belarus is reflected in the data collected on these countries by a number of international organizations, research institutions, and think tanks. The figures in this section include the meta-indicators studied for the three countries: level of democratization, political stability, and economic/ social development. Each of these meta-indicators includes multiple parameters that are jointly required for presentation of the holistic explanation of the two working hypotheses. The results of numerous statistical indicators mostly support the null hypothesis on the inability of democracy to prevent internal disturbances and foster economic and social development in Georgia, Ukraine, and Belarus. The data also confirms the positive hypothesis on the favorable influence of authoritarian resilience and third-party support in keeping internal and external political stability and contributing to the financial and social well-being of their populations.

Democratization.

The indicators put together in the "Democratization" category comprise general human rights and fundamental freedoms, as well as quality of governmental performance, including the degrees of efficiency and corruption. The annual report of Freedom House, *Freedom in the World 2013*, named Georgia and Ukraine as both "partially free" while Belarus as a "not free" country. By comparison, a "free country" is one with "open political competition, a climate of respect for civil liberties, significant independent civic life, and independent media."[45] The Polity IV dataset gave similar rankings: Georgia and Ukraine received polity scores (combined scores of institutionalized democracy and institutionalized autocracy) of 6 while Belarus was given a polity score of -7.[46]

By the majority of other parameters, Georgia is on top of the democracy scale. According to the *Press Freedom Index*, Georgia offers the best conditions for journalists to express their opinions (rank 100), followed by Ukraine (126) and Belarus (157).[47] The Worldwide Governance Indicators[48] presented by D. Kaufmann and M. Mastruzzi offer additional valuable insights into the understanding of the level of democratization of the three countries. The survey includes the following six indicators: Voice and Accountability, Political Stability/Absence of Violence/Terrorism, Government Effectiveness, Rule of Law, Regulatory Quality, and Control of Corruption. One of the most important indicators is "voice and accountability," which is the ability of citizens "to participate in selecting their government, as well as freedom of expression, freedom of association, and a free media."[49] In this category, Ukraine has the highest ranking (44.1 — a rounded percentile rank among all countries; ranges from 0 [lowest] to 100 [highest] very closely followed by Georgia [42.7]). On the contrary, Belarus offers the fewest opportunities for its citizens to express their views (7.1). However, by their performance in the "Political Stability" category, Belarus and Ukraine are practically close, with ranks of 41 and 42, respectively.

The least politically stable country, according to this survey, is Georgia, with the rank of 24.5. Paradoxically, the most effective governance is in Georgia (64.1) — in fact, it is five times more effective than in Belarus (12), and almost three times more than in Ukraine (24.9). Also, Georgia has the highest "Rule of Law" environment (48.8), while Belarus has the lowest capacity (14.7), with Ukraine being in between (25.1). The "Regulatory Quality" of the government is also the best in Georgia (70.8), which is almost twice as high as in Ukraine (32.5), and more than seven times higher than in Belarus (9.6).

Finally, the "Corruption" variable is of immense importance in understanding the dynamics of democratization. By the Worldwide Governance Indicators, Georgia is a champion of the "Control of Corruption" with a rank of 54.1, while Ukraine is the most corrupt country (17.2), and Belarus is in the middle (23). It is notable that the poll conducted by the Razumkov Center on corruption perception named the political sphere, the state, and the judiciary as the most corrupt out of all sectors of governance in Ukraine.[50] The *Transparency International Corruption Perception Index 2012* named Georgia as the least corrupt country of the three with a rating of 51, followed by Belarus (123), and Ukraine as the most corrupt country (144).

Another dataset, the World Development Indicators 2010, holds Georgia as the least corrupt of the three studied (by the percentage of firms offering informal payments to the public officials), with only 14.7 percent of companies paying bribes, and Ukraine as the most corrupt country with one third of the bribe-givers, with Belarus somewhat in between (26.1 percent). Finally, public perceptions on corruption also matter in the democratization processes. The Global

Corruption Barometer 2010/2011[51] holds three indicators in the study of public opinion in this particular aspect: perception of change, perception of most corrupt institutions, and perceptions of governments' anti-corruption efficiency. According to the Barometer, 78 percent of the respondents from Georgia believe that corruption decreased over the past 3 years, while most of respondents from Ukraine (63 percent) consider that corruption has not changed, and one-third feel that it has even increased. Lastly, 49 percent of the respondents in Belarus feel no change in the level of corruption.

Economic and Social Development.

Due to the significant differences in the countries' sizes and economic potentials, the data given in this section will focus on the per capita economic and social developmental parameters instead of giving cross-country comparisons in the levels of gross domestic products (GDPs) and the comparative aggregate economic growth. Overall, Belarus has the highest indicators of economic and social development, while Georgia, by many datasets, is the least developed, of the three countries, economically and socially. According to the World Development Indicators 2010,[52] gross national income (GNI) per capita in Belarus in 2010 was $5,950, with an overall GNI rank of 104. Belarus also has the lowest child mortality rates (17 per 1,000 live births in 1990 and only 6 in 2010), and the lowest maternal mortality ratio modeled estimate (15 per 100,000 live births in 2008). In addition, only 5.4 percent of the population of Belarus live below the national poverty line (national level in 2009), and the country has the best income or consumption distribution, i.e., the lowest 20 percent of the population possesses 9.2 percent of income distribution, while the highest 20 percent has 36.4 percent of income.

Notwithstanding the highest indicators of democracy, Georgia has had remarkably low economic and social performance over the years since its independence. The GNI per capita of the Georgian population in 2010 was only $2,690, with an overall GNI rank of 145. It is notable that Georgia has the highest child mortality rates among the three countries: 47 per 1,000 live births during the last year of the Soviet Union and 22 in 2010, with the worst maternal mortality ratio modeled estimate: 48 per 100,000 live births in 2008. Out of the three countries studied, Georgia has skyrocketing numbers of citizens living below the national poverty line at 24.7 percent (national level in 2009), and the worst income or consumption distribution: the lowest 20 percent of the population possesses 5.3 percent of income distribution, while the highest 20 percent has 47.2 percent of income distribution. The last figures are the indicators of the growing disproportionality between the wealthiest and the poorest layers of the population. This is, in itself, a barometer for worsening internal political stability, since large social disparities can lead to mass protests and political unrest.

Ukraine occupies a somewhat middle ground among the three countries with regards to its economic and social performance. The Ukrainian GNI per capita in 2010 was $3,000 — in between Belarus and Georgia — with an overall GNI rank of 136. The child mortality rates in Ukraine are also at midpoint: 21 per 1,000 live births in 1990 and 13 in 2010. The same situation can be found with the maternal mortality ratio modeled estimate: 26 per 100,000 live births in 2008. At the same time, Ukraine has the lowest percentage of citizens living below the national poverty line at 2.9 percent (national level in 2008), and the best income or consumption distribution: the lowest 20 percent of the population possesses 9.7 percent of income distribution, while the highest 20 percent has 36.3 percent of the income. The indicators are slightly higher than those for Belarus.

The three countries also differ significantly with regard to their investment climates, the facilitation of conducting businesses for the domestic and foreign entrepreneurs, as well as the overall dependency of foreign aid. The Heritage Foundation has ranked Ukraine the lowest among the three countries (161) and Georgia the highest (21), with Belarus being quite close to Ukraine (154)[53] in its *Index of Economic Freedoms*. According to the World Development Indicators, Georgia also has the least amount of foreign direct investments (FDIs) — $1.1 billion, surpassed by Belarus with its $4 billion and Ukraine with the highest FDIs at $7.2 billion.

Additional valuable inputs in understanding the domestic economic settings are contained in the data of the International Financial Corporation (IFC). The gap between the three countries with respect to doing business, protecting foreign investments and the dependence on foreign aid is quite striking. According to the IFC, the easiest country to do business with is Georgia (rank 9) while the most difficult is Ukraine (rank 137). Of the three countries, Georgia (rank 4) protects its investors the best. Ukraine, again, offers the least protection for foreign financial interests (rank 21).[54] Here, Belarus also occupies the middle grounds by these indicators. The IFC has given Georgia the highest indicators in the region of Eastern Europe and Central Asia, while Ukraine is the third from the bottom. Finally, Georgia depends the most upon foreign aid: it has 5.5 percent of the *GINI Index* of the foreign aid dependency ratio, whereas Ukraine and Belarus depend the least, with 0.3 percent and 0.5 percent, respectively. The high numbers of the population living off the support of the donor organizations in Georgia can be explained, among other factors, by two civil conflicts with the Abkhazian and South Ossetian secessionist regions starting from 1992, which led to about 280,000 internally displaced persons by 2012.[55]

Finally, participation of the countries in the globalization processes brings valuable insights about their economic and social development. The increased involvement in globalization may be a positive indicator for their overall market liberalization and favorable investment climate. From this point of view, the *KOF Index of Globalization 2012*,[56] produced by the Swiss Federal Institute of Technology, focuses on the economic, social, and political openness of the countries. The Index considers "economic globalization" as the combined indicator of actual monetary flows and restrictions. According to these parameters, the country most open to economic globalization is Georgia (rank 29) and the least open one is Belarus (rank 117), with Ukraine occupying the middle position (rank 61). "Social globalization" is considered as the sum of personal contacts (between the citizens of the countries in question and the rest of the world), information flows, and cultural proximity. According to this indicator, the most socially globalized country is Belarus (rank 60), followed by Ukraine (rank 69) and Georgia (rank 88). One of the reasons for such high social globalization of Belarus, notwithstanding its relative isolation from most of the outside world, is its considerably high integration into Russian economic and social networks.

Strong personal and family links between Belarusian and Russian populations, together with the Union State of Russia and Belarus, an entity with common political, economic, military, custom, currency, legal, humanitarian, and cultural space, trampolined Belarus to the most socially globalized country out of the three. Another explanation lies in the fact of frequent shopping trips of the Belarusians to the neighboring countries of the European Union (EU). As Alexander Lukashenka himself complained, Belarusians are spending $3 billion each year in their lucrative shopping in the EU. In the first half of 2013, there were over 3.8 million foreign trips registered to the EU, with the total population of Belarus of 9.5 million.[57]

Political Stability.

Most of the datasets prepared by the research institutions and public opinion polls named Georgia as the least stable internally (durability of state institutions to withstand internal disturbances) and externally (durability of state institutions to withstand external pressure). Belarus and Ukraine are significantly more stable by various parameters. The *Failed States Index 2013* developed annually by the Fund For Peace views the political stability through the prisms of three categories of variables: cultural (demographic pressure, refugees, group grievance, and human flight), economic (uneven development, poverty, and economic decline), and political (legitimacy of the state, political services, human rights, security apparatus, factorized elites, and external intervention).[58] In these combined categories, Georgia is ranked 51 of most failed states in the world, with the worst performance being in "group grievances," "state legitimacy," and "factionalized elites." From the point of view of external stability, the war with Russia pushed Georgia down to the rank of the 33rd most failed state in 2008. The least failed state is Ukraine, ranked 177, followed by Belarus (rank 81). A similar dataset, the *State Fragility Index*, developed in 2011 by Monty Marshall and Benjamin Cole, focuses on the combination of governance effectiveness and legitimacy parameters. The Index named Belarus as the most politically stable out of the three countries (rank 4) and Georgia as the least stable (rank 8).[59]

The civil wars Georgia suffered from represent the significant factor in decreasing the internal political stability of the country. According to *Eurostat 2012*, in 2010, Georgia was ranked 10 out of non-EU countries by the number of asylum seekers in the EU member-states.[60] Furthermore, in 2011, the *World Prison Population List* noted Georgia as having one of the highest prison populations per capita in the world (547 per 100,000). The same list noted Ukraine as having the lowest numbers of prisoners (338 per 100,000), with Belarus occupying the middle position out of the countries (381 prisoners per 100,000).[61]

Much along the same lines, the *2013 Global Peace Index* of the Institute of Economics and Peace, which includes multiple indicators for internal and external political stability, identified Georgia as the least peaceful country among the three studied here, ranking it 139. This is largely due to the war with Russia in 2008 and the continuous domestic rivalry between its multiple political forces. The best peace score (rank 96) was given to Belarus, while Ukraine was ranked 111. The Index explains the high stability score of Belarus by the phenomenon of "authoritarian resilience": strong centralized authority limiting any political and economic freedoms while suppressing the level of criminality, which is a visibly positive development. According to the Index, Belarus managed to suppress "[a]n independent class of wealthy businessmen able to exert a strong political influence. . . keeping corruption at lower levels than in neighbouring Russia and Ukraine."[62] Belarus also keeps a considerably high ratio of "internal security forces to population," which augments the authoritative resilience of its president by making the expression of free will a punishable venture. In Ukraine:

> [t]he main factors behind the decline in peacefulness . . . were a rise in perception of criminality under the presidency of Viktor Yanukovych . . . alongside a worsening of relations with an important neighbour, Russia.[63]

These two aspects negatively affected the ability of Ukraine to move up the peace ladder, which still put it high above Georgia with its unresolved conflicts.

The *Political Stability Index* of the Economist Intelligence Unit offers another look into the matter of internal durability of the governance regimes. The Index views political stability as "the level of threat posed to governments by social protest." The Index includes multiple variables that can be grouped, similarly to the *Failed States Index*, into political (history of post-independence and political instability, corruption, institutional trust, external political environment, regime types, and functionalism), economic (inequality, labor unrest, income growth, unemployment, and GDP per capita), and cultural (ethnic fragmentation, situation with minorities, and social provision). In 2009-10, according to the Index, the most politically stable country that thwarted public protests successfully was

Belarus (rank 124), while the most politically unstable one was Ukraine (rank 16) followed by Georgia (rank 73).[64] This is somewhat a deviation from the common pattern, which kept Georgia at the bottom of political stability. The Worldwide Governance Indicators produced by Kaufmann *et al.*[65] also name Belarus as the most politically stable (rank 41) country, and Georgia as having the lowest political stability (rank 24.5). At the same time, Georgia has the highest indicator for the regulatory quality (rank 70.8), government effectiveness (rank 64.1), and control of corruption (rank 54.1).

The level of participation of the countries in globalization can also be a measure of their external political stability. If a country is included in the processes of globalized economies, has wider political participation, and enjoys a higher level of social and cultural interactions, the more liberal and politically stable it will become. In addition to the economic and social globalization discussed previously, the KOF's *Index of Globalization* includes a third category, "political globalization." Political globalization is defined as the availability of foreign embassies and globalization inputs of the countries in question, such as memberships in international organizations, participation in the United Nations (UN) Security Council's missions, and membership in international treaties.[66] In this category, the most politically globalized country of the trio is Ukraine (rank 43), with Georgia and Belarus having somewhat closer standings: rank 139 and rank 145, respectively.

The high rank of Ukraine can be explained by its economic globalization via participating in the gas transit from Russia to Europe and family links with the large Ukrainian diaspora, mostly in Russia, but also slowly growing in the European countries and North America. The low ranking of Georgia and Belarus in the political globalization category can be explained by different reasons. Georgia's global political participation was somewhat stalled by its long-term domestic political turbulence, including the civil wars of 1992, 1992–94, and the recent war with Russia in 2008. The low standings of Belarus in political globalization, notwithstanding its strong economic and cultural performance in the form of economic remittances from and family links with Russia as well as frequent travels abroad, are due to the general closeness of its political environment, a vivid indicator of which is the ongoing disputes with Europe and the United States over human rights and political discrimination issues in Belarus, including the expulsion of ambassadors by Lukashenka.[67]

Does Public Opinion Matter?

With the purpose of further exploring the democracy/stability/development nexus in Ukraine, Georgia, and Belarus, a questionnaire was distributed among the social networks (country-specific groups in Facebook and LinkedIn as well as various University alumni networks) to study the opinion and views of citizens of these countries concerning the three variables of the current study. The poll included 27 questions split into three sections: Citizenship, Law, and Rights; Representative and Accountable Government; and Civil Society and Popular Participation. The questions were borrowed from and based on the *Democracy Assessment Guide of the International Institute of Democracy and Electoral Assistance*[68] and the U.S. Agency for International Development (USAID) *Guide to Rule of Law.*[69] The response levels to the questionnaire in these three countries are characteristic of the high levels of political activity of domestic policy in some and the chronic apathy in others: 157 people participated in the questionnaire in Georgia, 64 in Ukraine, and only 13 in Belarus.

Citizenship, Law and Rights.

Almost half of the Ukrainian respondents think that the rule of law is not provided throughout the country, whereas 44 percent are neutral on this question. The responses among the Belarusian pool are practically the same: 54 percent believe that the rule of law is not effective, and only 18 percent consider that the level of the rule of law is acceptable. Of Georgian respondents, 28 percent gave positive answers to this question, while 57 percent are on the middle ground. An overwhelming majority of the respondents in Ukraine (78 percent) and Belarus (64 percent) do not consider their country to have an effective separation of the branches of government, including independence of the courts from judiciary and executive powers. The answers among Georgian participants were split between those who are of a neutral opinion on this matter (43 percent) and those who do not consider the branches to be independent from each other (41 percent).

Only 1.6 percent of the respondents in Ukraine have confidence in the legal system of their country to deliver fair and effective justice, while most of them (73 percent) think that the legal system is not effective. In Belarus, the situation is different: 27 percent of participants trust their legal system, whereas 27 percent and 18 percent have low and the lowest trust, with an additional 27 percent occupying the middle position on this question. The numbers of those who trust and mistrust the legal system in Georgia are almost equal: 24 percent and 27 percent, respectively, with 48 percent having the middle opinion.

About half of the Ukrainian respondents think that the situation with democracy and human rights is bad or very bad (25 percent, respectively), and only 20 percent believe that the democracy level is high, and that human rights are provided by the government, with one third neutral on this question. More people in Belarus (63 percent combined) are of a negative opinion of their government's ability to protect their rights, while only 9 percent consider that their rights are protected, with 27 percent having a neutral opinion on this question. A remarkable 53 percent of Georgian respondents think that human rights are better protected now than 10 years ago, and only 12 percent believe that the situation has changed for the worse.

When human rights are translated into specifics of freedoms of movement, expression, association, and assembly, the highest number of the Ukrainian respondents (over 41 percent) think that they are more or less provided; over 21 percent believe that the situation with these rights is good, and only 33 percent of them think that these rights are not safeguarded. The Belarusian respondents are mostly of an opposite opinion: a combined 54 percent do not consider that these rights are provided or are not fulfilled by the state; a little more than 33 percent of them are of a neutral opinion on this question; and only 9 percent are satisfied with the situation. Of the Georgian respondents, 46 percent positively evaluate the condition with these rights in Georgia, 40 percent more are content with the situation, while 12 percent think that these rights are provided for effectively and for all residents. The rate of negative and positive responses in Ukraine is balanced on the issue of freedom of speech: 29.6 percent of them are satisfied with it, 22.2 percent are not, while 46 percent consider the level as acceptable. Of the Belarusian respondents, 63 percent believe that freedom of speech is not provided in the country, and another 27 percent are of a neutral opinion on this subject. The situation is drastically different in Georgia: a combined total of 46 percent consider the situation with freedom of speech as good and very good, and 35 percent are of a neutral opinion.

The responses to the questions on another set of human rights — freedom of religion, language, and cultural rights — were not positive in Ukraine: 75 percent believe that the situation with these rights ranges from bad to very bad. On the contrary, 45 percent of the Belarusian respondents consider the situation with these rights as good, and 36 percent think it is acceptable. The same occurs in Georgia: 61 percent of those questioned think that the situation is good, 28 percent are of the middle opinion on this question, and only 10 percent think it is bad.

The views of the Ukrainian respondents were almost equally split (20 percent each) between those who think that individuals and organizations working to improve human rights are free from harassment and intimidation and those who believe they are harassed, while the rest occupies the middle ground on this question. In Belarus, however, most of the respondents (72 percent combined) believe that human rights activists are harassed. The situation was, again, different in Georgia, where, according to 45 percent of the respondents, human rights activists are mostly free from intimidation in fulfilling their duties; another 43 percent think that the situation is acceptable. The situation with economic freedoms in Ukraine is considered bad by 40 percent of respondents, very bad by 13.3 percent, and good only by 11.6 percent. In Belarus, however, most of those questioned (54 percent) take the middle ground on this matter, and the remaining are equally spread between opposing opinion spectrums. A similar situation is in Georgia: 44 percent of the respondents have a middle opinion on the matter of economic freedoms, 31 percent believe that condition with these freedoms is good, and 24 percent are not satisfied with the condition of economic freedoms.

Finally, most of the Ukrainian respondents are either somewhat unhappy (40 percent) or not satisfied at all (44 percent) with the level of economic development of Ukraine. The situation is different in Belarus: 45 percent of the respondents think that the economic development of their country is on an average level, and there is a balance between those who are satisfied and dissatisfied with the performance of the Belarusian economy. Most of the Georgian respondents occupy the middle ground on this matter; another 24 percent are satisfied with the economic development, while 32 percent are not happy with the situation.

Representative and Accountable Government.

The majority of Ukrainian (up to 60 percent) and Belarusian (89 percent) respondents believe that the elections in their respective countries have not become more transparent over the last decade. The situation is drastically different in Georgia: 90 percent of respondents consider the elections procedure to have significantly improved over the past 10 years. In Ukraine,

40 percent of participants think that the opposition parties and NGOs are moderately free in organizing themselves, whereas the numbers of those on the opposing spectrum of the opinion (fully free/not fully free) are almost equal: 25.5 percent and 29 percent, correspondingly. Most of the Belarusian respondents consider their opposition parties and NGOs to be either oppressed (22 percent) or highly oppressed (44 percent). In Georgia, the situation is different: a combined 55 percent believe that their opposition parties and NGOs are free from prosecutions, and 30 percent think their freedom is on an average level.

Most of the respondents from Ukraine are either somewhat not satisfied (46 percent) or mostly unsatisfied (18 percent) with their last elections, whereas 28.5 percent of them occupy the middle ground on this issue, and only 8 percent of them combined are either fully or partially satisfied with the elections. The respondents from Belarus are most dissatisfied with the elections (64 percent combined). On the contrary, most of the Georgian respondents are either satisfied (40 percent) or very satisfied (31 percent) with the recent elections, and another 20 percent occupy the middle position on this question. The overwhelming majority of Ukrainian respondents do not trust their government to some degree (62.5 percent fully and 26.8 percent partially), with only 1.8 percent having full trust in it. The numbers of those trusting their government are higher in Belarus (11 percent fully trust, 33 percent partially trust, and 33 percent do not trust). The Georgian respondents were almost equally split between those who do not trust their government (27 percent) and those who do (33 percent), with the remaining 40 percent having a middle opinion on this matter.

On the question of access by the citizens to government information, the majority of the Ukrainian respondents think that the situation is on a moderate level (49 percent), whereas 33 percent think that citizens cannot get access to information. Most of the Belarusian respondents (44 percent) occupy the middle ground on this question; 33 percent of them share their Ukrainian counterparts' views on partial access to the information, and 11 percent think that they are deprived of such information. Half of the Georgian respondents are of a middle opinion on this question, and another 33 percent are satisfied with the access to governmental information. Most of those questioned in Ukraine (79 percent combined) think that police and security services are not accountable to the public, and so do 55 percent of their Belarusian counterparts. At the same time, 22 percent of them think that police and security services are somewhat accountable. In Georgia, 33 percent of respondents consider police somewhat accountable, and 12 percent think they are fully accountable to the public, whereas 37 percent keep accountability at the average level.

Of the Ukrainian respondents, 43 percent believe the crime level in their country to be on a moderate level; 29 percent and 13 percent think that it is somewhat high and very high, correspondingly. Among the Belarusian respondents, 44 percent think that the crime level is moderate, 33 percent think it is low, and 22 percent believe that is it high. In Georgia, most of those questioned (54 percent) think the crime level is low, 31 percent consider it acceptable, and only 13 percent think it is high. Most of the respondents in Ukraine (87 percent) think that businesses influence public policy, and so do their Georgian counterparts (60 percent), whereas in Belarus the majority (67 percent) believes that politics is free from the influences of large corporations.

Finally, on the question on corruption in the government, 20 percent and 35.7 percent in Ukraine consider public officials and public services as somewhat corrupt or very corrupt. In Belarus, the majority (44 percent) think that corruption is on a moderate level. Most of the Georgian respondents (41 percent) take a middle ground on this question; 36 percent believe their civil servants are free from corruption.

Civil Society and Popular Participation.

Of the Ukrainian respondents, 42 percent believe that the independence of mass media from the government is on an average level, and another 40.7 percent of them think that it is not independent. In Belarus, these numbers are skewed towards the negative spectrum: 55.5 percent and 11 percent, respectively, consider mass media somewhat dependent and very dependent on the government. In Georgia, the situation is similar: 43 percent of the respondents view mass media as dependent on the government and only 21% think it is independent.

The question on efficiency of media in investigating government and private corporations divided the pool of Ukrainian respondents in half: 20 percent are on opposite sides of the spectrum, while 52.7 percent are neutral on this issue. The same response rate in Ukraine can be found on the question of freedom of journalists from restrictive laws, harassment, and intimidation. The respondents from Belarus are more pessimistic in their estimates of media efficiency: overall, 77 percent of them think that mass media is not efficient. In Georgia, the majority of respondents was either pessimistic (34 percent) or took the middle ground (43 percent) on the investigative ability of journalists. The situation with journalists' freedom in Belarus is radically different: an overwhelming 88 percent of respondents believe that their journalists work under constant harassment by the government. The political polarization in Georgia is also evident in this question: while 40 percent are of a neutral opinion on media liberty, 32 percent think that journalists are harassed and another 28 percent think they are not harassed.

Of Ukrainians, 49 percent are of a neutral opinion on independence of voluntary associations, citizen groups, and social movements from the government, whereas 38 percent and 5 percent of them think that they are somewhat independent and fully independent from government pressure. Their Georgian counterparts are of a different standing: 43 percent have a middle view on this issue, while 43 percent think that they are very independent from the government. The Belarusian respondents are of a completely different opinion on this question: 66 percent view the third sector as not independent from their government.

From the point of view of external political stability, most of the Ukrainian respondents think that their country is somewhat independent (49 percent) or fully independent (14.5 percent) from the influence of other countries on its domestic political affairs. The Belarusian response rate is almost the same: 55.5 percent think that their country is somewhat independent, and 11 percent consider it fully independent from outside influences. In Georgia, too, most respondents (54 percent) believe their country is free from outside influences, and another 34 percent are of a middle opinion.

The future internal political stability for each country was evaluated quite differently within the three countries. Of the Ukrainian respondents, 58 percent feel that significant political changes will happen to Ukraine in the next five years, whereas the rest believe in political stability without any major transformations. Georgians are of a more radical view: 78 percent anticipate significant changes in the political life of their country. Their Belarusian counterparts are of exactly the opposite opinion: 67 percent do not expect any notable political change to happen in Belarus in the next 5 years. Such an outlook in Ukraine is due to, perhaps, the fact that most of those questioned prefer political freedoms (69 percent) to economic stability, which argues for an increase in the level of political activity of the masses over the coming years. In Georgia, too, 63 percent prefer politically free rather than economically stable. In Belarus, the situation is opposite: 56 percent prefer economic freedoms to political liberties.

POLITICAL CULTURE AS AN IDENTITY CONSTRUCT

The responses to the questionnaire reflect the interplay between the levels of democratization, political stability, and economic development in the target countries. Political culture is the meta-variable that glues together the other variables and affects the behavior of the institutional actors and their opinions regarding specific aspects of their respective governance regime. It permeates the very core of the societal fabric and profoundly impacts the ways the actors respond to internal and external disturbances of their political environment. Political culture is a very complex phenomenon. It does not appear overnight. It is a complex product of convoluted interactions of the actors at the political, economic, and cultural layers intertwining the social fabric. In order to understand the current political settings in Ukraine, Georgia, and Belarus, which influenced the course of democratization of their societies after independence, it is necessary to go back in their histories. The circumstances that led to the creation of the complex phenomenon of political culture are pivotal in understanding the responses of the three nations to the changing domestic and international environs.

Political Culture.

In the present context, the notion of political culture goes beyond Douglas North's definition of culture, which is a "language-based conceptual framework for encoding and interpreting the information that the lenses are presenting to the brain."[70] Dittmer defines political culture as "a system of political symbols . . . nest[ing] in a more inclusive system that we might term 'political communication',"[71] which is deeply embedded in the identities of the actors reflected in their political behavior. Political behavior, according to Claude Ake, is:

> ubiquitous. Members of society behave politically insofar as, in obeying or disobeying the laws of the society, they support or undermine the power stratification system.[72]

David Laitin and Aaron Wildavski view political culture as a three-prong phenomenon: it instills "points of concern to be debated"; it guides people "by the symbols of their culture and is instrumental in using culture to gain wealth and power"; and it contains the symbols, which "must be interpreted in full ethno-graphic context."[73]

For the purposes of the present research, political culture is defined as "modes of responses of institutional actors to challenges emanating from internal and external environments." Based on that definition, political culture becomes, essentially, the symbolic media of political behavior—what Stephen Chilton calls "all publicly common ways of relating within the collectivity"[74]—in other words, the ways in which the institutional actors interact with their governance regimes and react to the presented political agendas, both domestic and international. Symbolic communications between the institutional actors within the specific governance regimes make political culture the product of their identities.

On the domestic level, political culture includes the sets of behavioral responses of the actors towards the changes of their governance regimes. The same applies to the level of international system, only in this case, the changes in the governance are substituted by the fluctuations of the regional and/or global environment, depending on the roles the countries in question play in it. On either of these levels, changes occur on the institutional level and follow the pace of normative "lifecycles." These lifecycles involve three stages defined by Martha Finnemore and Kathryn Sikkink as "norm emergence," "norm cascading," and "norm internalization."[75]

The normative change cycle starts with appearance of a norm either from inside, for example, the inception of human rights in England's *Magna Carta* in the 13th century and the French Revolution of 1789, or from outside, such as the post-colonial and post-imperial governance transformations following the imperial collapses and based on externally proposed governance models. Gradually, the change of a norm in one sphere (for instance, in law enforcement) leads to normative spillovers in other areas (healthcare, education, urban planning, social security, etc.) starting to involve increased numbers of institutional actors. The final stage of the democratic normative lifecycle — when a norm becomes a part of the political culture of a nation, an inherent component of its "moral fit," and the core of its national identity — is the lengthiest process of all since it affects not only specific institutions, but also the whole complexity.

For the process of institutional change of political regimes to be successful and (more importantly) durable, it should transcend through the institutional actors with relatively insignificant interruptions. The outcomes of all the three stages of the normative lifecycle of institutional change depend directly on the political cultures of the target societies and how receptive they are to change. Political culture can be lenient and well receptive to political change, or it can be rigid and somewhat immune to institutional transformations. In the first case, the institutional change happens somewhat smoothly because of its acceptance by relatively high numbers of institutional actors. The rigid cultures, where the actors who prefer institutional statism to change, slow lifecycles.

THREE HISTORICAL NARRATIVES

Political cultures of different nations are not homogenous inasmuch as their identities are different. Political cultures are not created overnight; they are born out of centuries of human development and interactions with the neighboring societies and polity. Ukraine, Georgia, and Belarus had similar historical conditions existing prior to their independence and even before Communist rule, which draw parallels between their overall socio-political and economic developmental levels. Nevertheless, there is a significant diversity among their political cultures influencing the current levels of democratization, political stability, and economic development.

Historical Ukraine.

Historically molded, Ukrainian identity is comprised, according to Sergei Shtukarin, of triple constructs: "national," where its bearer reacts positively to the maxima "Ukraine for Ukrainians"; "civil," which implies loyalty to Ukraine's statehood regardless of ethnic background; and "alien" identity, which regards both Ukrainian ethnicity and statehood as foreign.[76] Similarly, as Serhy Yekelchuk notes, the Ukrainian national identity engulfed three components, being "a direct descendant of medieval Kyivan Rus, the 17th-century Cossack polity, and the 1918–1920 Ukrainian People's Republic."[77] Current geographic divide in the Ukrainian society into the pro-European west and pro-Russian east was born of the centuries of interactions with both sides of the bipolar identity equation. Ukraine, with its historical core of the Kyivan Rus' which gave birth to the medieval Slavic fiefdoms, represents the basis for common Eastern Slavic identity[78] and was the center which the future Russian Empire would build around, but just at the outskirts of it.[79] The name "Ukraine" in Eastern Slavic dialects means "at the edge," the "borderland." Ukraine had its short period of independence during medieval times in the form of the Galicia-Volhynia political entity in the 13th and 14th centuries, which Ukrainian historian Stefan Tomashivsky named as "the first undeniably Ukrainian state."[80]

In the 15th and 16th centuries, a part of present-day Ukraine was included into the powerful Polish-Lithuanian Commonwealth,[81] after which some of its western territories became semi-independent under the rule of the Cossacks, who were "Orthodox men roaming the steppes, and . . . famously independent minded."[82] Cossacks were the military regiments gathered in Zaporojskaya Sech' who pledged no allegiance to their neighbors, be it the Polish-Lithuanian union, the Ottoman Empire, the Crimean Khanate, or Moscowia, the modern Russia. The governance regime in Sech' could be named as an embryonic democracy with some sort of separation of responsibilities between the elected Hetman (the leader) and the Rada (the equivalent of the modern Parliament), which was a consultative body, as well as the equal voice given to every Cossack. A century later, in 1710, Sech' produced one of the first prototypes of a modern-day democratic constitution under Hetman Orlyk,[83] with real attributes of democracy, including the separation of powers and an elective governance style.

However, it was they, the Cossacks, who, after the bloody defeat by the Polish army in 1651, asked Alexei I, Tsar of Moscovia, to accept them under his protection.[84] They were seeking a temporary military alliance, fearing the ultimate subjugation by the Polish reign. The initial arrangements provided for mutual loyalty of Cossacks and Alexei I, wide autonomy, and keeping of internal composition of Ukraine. Later on, however, these accords were broken, and Moscovia totally subordinated the land it initially promised to defend (temporarily) from outside enemies. This marked the period of Ukrainian history under Russian rule, which transitioned to Soviet governance after the October Revolution of 1917. Ukraine did have its independence, though, in the form of the Ukrainian People's Republic in 1918 and the West Ukrainian People's Republic, which joined the former in 1919 with the loss of its territory to Poland, Romania, and Czechoslovakia in the Polish-Ukrainian war of June 1919. Ukrainian independence, however, turned out to be short-lived, and Ukraine was ultimately vanquished by the Soviet Army in mid-summer 1920, creating the Ukrainian Soviet Socialist Republic.

Historical Georgia.

Situated "at a major commercial crossroads and among several power neighbors"[85] — not all of them friendly — right in the middle of the Great Silk Road, a halfway point between the East and the West, Georgian identity and culture has been historically exposed to the influences of diverse cultures, religions, languages, and mostly authoritarian governance regimes of the regional powers. The history of Georgia precipitates with foreign conquerors with direct and indirect reigns — Byzantine, Seljuk, Ottoman Turkey, Sassanid Persia, Arabs, and Mongols[86] — up until 1783, when eastern Georgia, followed by the western part of the country, were incorporated into the Russian Empire.[87] Notwithstanding the heavy external political pressure and centuries of political subordination, Georgia remained a country with unchanged Christian beliefs, unique language (with its own written alphabet), and a very specific set of cultural traits.

The end of the Russian Empire as a result of the October Revolution of 1917 gave a glimpse of hope to the Georgian polity, which soon established the first true modern independent country. However, what appeared to be the start of its independent existence on a par with the regional actors in reality was only a short intermission between the two empires—the Russian one and the Soviet Union one in the making. In 1921, Georgia, along with its immediate Caucasian neighbors, Armenia and Azerbaijan, was conquered by the Russian military[88] and forcefully made a member of the Transcaucasian Socialist Federated Republic. Fifteen years later, this entity dissolved, with its members becoming separate, but not sovereign, republics within the Soviet Union.

Historical Belarus.

Creation of the Belarus nation dates back to the migration of the Eastern Slavic tribes in the 6th through 8th centuries further eastwards to the borders of contemporary Belarus. The name "Belarus," or "White Russia," as noted by Jan Zaprudnik:

> originated in the 12th century and initially designated various parts of northwestern Russia or Ukraine. Since the 14th century, it has also been applied to eastern territories of present-day Belarus.[89]

Similar to Ukraine, Belarus had its first independent states of Polatsk, Turai, and Navahradak between the 9th and 13th centuries.[90] In later centuries, largely owing to the Mongol conquest of the Kyivan Rus' in 1240, the lands populated by the Belarusian tribes were taken over by, first, the Grand Duchy of Lithuania, and later in the 16th century by the Polish-Lithuanian Commonwealth. The Commonwealth lasted until the late-18th century when, as a result of the three partitions of Poland, according to Andrew Wilson, "Belarus was swallowed almost whole by the Romanov Empire...."[91] — the growing strength of Tsarist Russia.

With the long history of Belarus, scholars stumble upon multiple roadblocks of defining Belarusian identity: is it Russian, similar to Russian, or something else? Historically, its origins, as Serhii Plokhy notes, "the Belarusian [identity] was based on the Ruthenian identity that had previously developed in the Grand Duchy of Lithuania but failed to produce distinct identity in modern times."[92] Among the possible reasons for the Belarus identity limbo was the systematic policy of *Russification* of the Tsarist rule, which was a part of the grand objective to de-Polonize the eastern Slavic lands within the Russian Empire and, thus, to pave the road for the gradual spread of Eastern Orthodoxy replacing Western Catholicism. In the push to eradicate the national consciousness of the Belarusians, Russian Tsar Nicolai I prohibited the usage of the term "Belarusia" and renamed the land the "North-Western Territory," simultaneously banning the use of Belarusian as a distinct language in the 1840s.[93] At the same time, the spread of socialist ideology in the Russian Empire and the industrial revolution had together emancipated the national self-consciousness of some of its nations, including the Belarusians. Following the defeat of Germany in World War I, the Belarusian Soviet Socialist Republic was created in 1918, marking an era of new communist governance, which, after the end of 1922 (the official inception of the USSR), received the name "Sovietization."

Under the Soviet Union.

During the Soviet period, and even for quite some time after the USSR dissolution, the political cultures of its former republics were viewed from outside as somewhat uniform, as either all "Soviet" or all "Russian." They were considered as parts of the gigantic ex-communist monolithic society with homogenous norms, rules, and practices. There was, indeed, a fair amount of truth in having such an approach to the nations willingly or forcefully brought under Soviet rule. The process of conversion of the identities of the multiethnic population speaking different languages and having quite diverse (and somewhat alien to each other) cultural traits and customs into a uniform one had the purpose of creating a single Soviet political culture.

The primary aim of the Soviet Union can be presented as the process of cultural homogenization of the Soviet nations. The manual on *Cultural policy in the Byelorussian Soviet Socialist Republic*, as quoted by David Marples, identified three stages of the Sovietization process. The purpose of the first one was "to introduce a 'social attitude' among the population and to develop the ideological base of the working class."[94] The pinnacle of this endeavor, as rendered by its mastermind, Joseph Stalin, was:

> [t]he flourishing of the cultures, which are national in form and socialist in content, under the dictatorship of the proletariat in one country with the purpose of merging them into a single socialist (both in form and content) culture with a common language.[95]

This was, however, illogical in its core; while the aim of Sovietization was eradication of the ethnic/national characteristics of its member-nations and creation of the one-size-fits-all Soviet identity, the process itself encouraged existence and, even more so, fermentation of national consciousness.

The politics of Russification had an important part in the overall Sovietization process (conversion of citizens into *Homo sovieticus*), but it was conducted quite subtly and mostly had to deal with the promotion of the Russian language as the medium of inter-republican communication while keeping the national identities alive. In Belarus, for example, the policy of *korenizaciya* ("indigenization") gave the Russian language the status of the "second" language after Belarusian, while Belarusian retained its official language status.[96] In Georgia, according to J. Parsons, the:

> Soviet policy has given active encouragement to the *rastsvet* or flourishing of Georgian culture (as of that of the other nationalities) in the belief that by providing for both the socio-economic development of the republics and for political and cultural equality, attachment to national differences would, by itself, subside.[97]

As a result, neither the Georgian language nor the Georgian orthodoxy was stifled by early Soviet authorities. After Stalin, an ethnic Georgian was deposed post-mortem from his "personality cult," and the anti-Stalin campaign started, which was viewed by many Georgians as anti-Georgian. In 1978, the Russian language was elevated to the level of official language along with Georgian, which was vehemently rejected by the Georgian establishment.

In Ukraine, this process, according to Anna Reid, was stricter than in either of the two communist republics in question. Reid identified a number of reasons for the more rigorous Russification of Ukraine:

comparatively early existence under the Soviet geopolitical umbrella and the denial of the unique Ukrainian identity by Russian nationalists. According to Reid:

> Russians deny their [Ukrainians'] existence. Ukrainians are a 'non-historical nation,' the Ukrainian language is a joke dialect. . . . The very closeness of Ukrainian and Russian culture, the very subtlety of the differences between them, is an irritation.[98]

The denial of the ethnic uniqueness of Ukrainians, which Chaim Kaufman considers as the "strongest" identity of all,[99] became an integral part of the systematic nationalism policy towards Ukraine in the Soviet Union. This process, however, was not uniquely Soviet. Similar to the Belarusian language ban, it started when Ukraine was a part of the Russian Empire. The so-called *Valuevskiy Cirkulyar* (Circular Letter of Valuev) by the Minister of Interior, and Ems Ukaz (in 1863 and 1876, respectively) banned the use of the Ukrainian language and dialects in the western provinces.

A somewhat lackadaisical approach to Soviet Russification in Belarus and Georgia, as opposed to the relentless take on Ukraine, can be explained by the differences in the views of Moscow on these nations. In Belarus, the lax Russification could be explained, among other reasons, by the fact that the ruling Russian elite of the Soviet Union felt little urge to change the Belarusian identity, since they largely viewed it as Russian by definition. In Georgia, the situation was on the opposite side of the spectrum of Russification policies. The Georgian language and culture were so alien to the Slavic language and culture that complete Russification efforts were not rationally justifiable. Besides, similar to the Belarusians, the Georgian elite and intelligentsia already had been integrated tightly within the Russian environment for several centuries after joining the Russian Empire, which made the process of socialization between these nations easy. Last, but not least, is the personality of Joseph Stalin, *quis fabricates* of the Soviet policy on nationalities, who, being an ethnic Georgian, was strict with the Georgian establishment in political matters[100] but was somewhat lenient toward the expression of national self-consciousness.

Ukraine occupies the middle ground in the Russification policies in the three countries. Ukraine in its current territory appeared only in 1947 (excluding Crimea); the two parts of the country were growing in different political cultures—those of Russian and Austro-Hungarian Empires, respectively. On the one hand, although the Ukrainians were always tightly associated with the Russians themselves, the former felt strong nationalistic impulses coming from the Ukrainian elites, especially from its western parts. De-Ukrainization, including eradication of the Ukrainian language and culture, also embraced the identity factor. These policies extended far beyond mere linguistic subordination; since Ukraine historically was considered a core of the Russian identity, having this history belong to another nation or being narrated in another language would mean deprecation of the Russian identity. As Zbigniew Brzezinski rightly observed, "[W]ithout Ukraine, Russia ceases to be an empire, but with Ukraine suborned and then subordinated, Russia automatically becomes as empire."[101]

There was, thus, a political reasoning behind the identity denial: The stronger the Russian/Soviet cultural linkages were with the Ukrainians, the stronger the cultural cleavage between Ukrainians and the Western world, especially with its immediate neighbors—Poland and Lithuania. The systematic identity denial by the Russian imperial and then Soviet authorities created long-lasting stigmatization in Ukraine and had its part in the regional divide in Ukraine. The process of Sovietization in Ukraine had another significantly more tragic side. As a result of the policies of *dekulakization* (resettlement of the wealthy peasants to the northern territories) and *collectivization* (expropriation of the land and its transfer into the collective ownership, basically, abolition of private property),[102] nearly 5 million people[103] vanished in what became known as the Ukrainian holocaust, or the "Holodomor."[104]

With the dissolution of the Soviet Union, the common political identity of the three nations as "Soviets" slowly began to vanish. In early-1990s, Georgia, Ukraine, and Belarus were suddenly exposed to the completely new international and domestic political realities and challenges of the independent statehood demanding some sort of reaction on the parts of their newly established national elites. Their responses to the new international environment were, however, quite predictable. Without the proper institutional knowledge of democratic practices and procedures, the newly created states used past experiences of communist bureaucracies merged with existing democratic institutional designs to build the bridges into their future. Lundell noted the phenomenon in the following passage: "Autocratic continuance [there] is largely due to the Soviet legacy. One-party communism has in many former Soviet republics been replaced by absolute presidential power."[105] By 1992, Georgia, Ukraine, and Belarus slid into the quagmire of stagnant ex-communist leadership with varying degrees of post-Soviet autocratic governance, but with signs of democracy embodied in such formative practices as elections and institutions of governance. Such a governing anomaly led to a volatile state in the domestic polity, and in some extreme cases, in grave turmoil.

Independent Ukraine.

Ukraine had its share of domestic problems during the early years of its independence. The anti-communist national self-determination group People's Movement of Ukraine, or the *Rukh*, according to Anders, Aslund, and Michael McFaul, "served as an umbrella group for hundreds of local and national civic, cultural, political, and human rights organizations"[106] in the late-1980s. The Rukh organized mass rallies calling for the removal of the communist party bosses and for the ultimate democratization of the country. It culminated in setting up a human chain from Kyiv to Lviv in 1990 in commemoration of the short-lived Ukrainian independence in 1919 and to show the unity of the Ukrainian lands from the west to the east. Right after independence, however, the Rukh lost its momentum and popular influence among particularly radical institutional actors, giving way to the old communist apparatchiks.

The first president of Ukraine, Leonid Kravchuk, a former communist bureaucrat and member of the Ukrainian Politburo, was at the time of independence the speaker of the Verkhovna Rada (the Parliament). Kravchuk managed to transform "himself within less than 2 years from communist ideological policeman to national communist leader and . . . Ukraine's first president and national leader."[107] Although Ukraine received large economic and industrial resources from the Soviet Union as a part of its independence inheritance, this potential appeared to be obsolete and ill fit under the burden of independent existence. Skyrocketing inflation, coupled with the completely severed tentacles of the command-and-controlled economy centrally providing both the demand and supply line for the Soviet economy and thoughtless economic reforms, led to rapid economic downfall, including hyperinflation, severe GNP crush, corruption in the privatization policies, and the chronic budgetary deficit.[108]

In 1994, Leonid Kuchma replaced Kravchuk as a result of the fierce presidential pre-election battle and immediately started the painful process of economic stabilization of Ukraine. The results of the market liberalization reforms were the decrease of the country's budgetary deficit, inflation, shrinking of public spending, increase of the GDP (although still lower than pre-1990 levels), and price stabilization.[109] With this, Kuchma's activities were aimed at attracting foreign loans, coping with balance of payments, and dispersion of credits, in other words, postponing the resolution of problems of real market reforms for an undefined future.[110] Also, Kuchma was not free from preferential political and economic regionalism and nepotism. He was accused by some in Ukraine of allegedly ordering the kidnapping and assassination of local journalist Georgiy Gongadze (coincidentally an ethnic Georgian), who was famous for his anti-corruption articles.[111] The "competitive authoritarianism" type of governance developed under Kuchma where:

> democratic institutions exist and are regarded as principal means of obtaining and exercising political authority, but powerholders violate those rules so often that the regime fails to meet minimum democratic standards.[112]

The regime was, thus, not fully authoritarian but not democratic enough to allow for the free and fair expressions of the institutional actors of their political preferences.

The eventual failure of Kuchma's regime, notorious for corruption, is largely considered as the main precondition for the Orange Revolution in 2005. The public protests staged as a response to mass election fraud allegedly committed by the forces acting against the presidential pro-western runner-up Viktor Yushchenko enjoyed wide popular support. The regional split was also present here; while Yushchenko was mostly considered a pro-Western politician and enjoyed the support of western and central Ukraine, Viktor Yanukovych, then Prime Minister of Ukraine and the principal contender in the presidential elections in November 2004, had his electorate largely based in eastern pro-Russian Ukraine. The democratic part of the Ukrainian society predominantly viewed Yanukovych as a "Kuchma reincarnate" with the same Soviet-style bureaucracy and Kuchma's backing. Yushchenko, who, by independent exit polls won by a margin of 10 percent in the second round, was put behind Yanukovych by the Central Election Committee. This sparked mass protest rallies by Yushchenko's supporters in Kyiv and elsewhere in Ukraine[113] except for its eastern regions. The third round of elections held in December confirmed Yushchenko's victory.

The promises of political change and economic revival made by incoming President Yushchenko appeared to be short-lived and the democratic path too difficult to continue. Because of internal struggle between powerful political and economic forces, Yushchenko appointed Yanukovych as Prime Minister in

2006. As a result of subsequent presidential elections, 4 years later Yanukovych became the President of the country,[114] marking an almost 180-degree reversal from the volatile democracy to possible stable but stagnant rule. The result of the elections further widened the regional political divide in Ukraine on the pro-democratic West and the pro-Russian East. A clear sign of the fluctuations of the bifurcate political course of Ukraine is the May 2013 conclusion of the memorandum on obtaining the observer status in the Customs Union of the Eurasian Economic Community and the forthcoming agreement with the EU about the free trade zone in November 2013. The latter, to his credit, was initiated by Yanukovych, who is struggling to keep balance between the two gravity centers.

The first direction is towards Vladimir Putin's pet project of *in vitro* testing for the possible reanimation of the Soviet Union. The second direction is toward closer integration with the democratic communities. Ukraine does not want to "upset" both sides of the equation; according to Suzdalcev, Ukraine:

> wants to have all the benefits of the Customs Union but is not going to join it; instead, it wants to enter the European Union.[115]

These are, essentially, mutually exclusive steps, which would define the foreign political alignment of Ukraine for generations to come.

Notwithstanding these oscillations, Ukraine continues to receive foreign support. According to the USAID "Greenbook" website, Ukraine received approximately U.S.$1.7 billion in economic assistance[116] with an additional U.S.$103.593 million in 2012, a planned U.S.$104.407 million for 2013, with another

U.S.$95.271 million planned for 2014.[117] Ukraine is also a recipient of European aid; in 2011, the EU provided €30 million (euros) as an:

> assistance package to support the Ukrainian government in their institutional reform efforts in several key areas, including the Deep and Comprehensive Free Trade area, sanitation, state aid, and migration.[118]

Independent Georgia.

Early years of independence for Georgia were marked by the civil war against its first president, Zviad Gamsakhurdia, who came to power on the nationalistic and chauvinistic wave. Gamsakhurdia, whom Per Gahrton described as a "tactical fanatic," "was an attractive and even efficient leader and a symbol of national liberation movement . . . [but] a catastrophe as executive administrator and president."[119] Gamsakhurdia's reign proved to be short-lived when a significant part of his own close entourage and some military regiments revolted in early-1992. The resulting coup d'état paved the road to Georgian leadership for Eduard Shevardnadze, a mastodon of Soviet politics. By that time, Shevardnadze, probably the most well-known Georgian to the world outside of the former Soviet space, already ruled the republic from 1972 to 1985 as the first secretary of the Georgian Communist Party.

Shevardnadze re-entered Georgian politics first as the Chairman of the State Council, then Chairmen of Parliament from 1992–95, and finally its president from 1995 until the Rose Revolution of 2003. His early years in power were notable for the rollercoaster of internal Georgian political preferences and the disastrous economic condition. Most of Georgian economic potential in Soviet times was centered on the summer Black Sea resorts, tea production, citruses, and wine making, most of which were located in western Georgia, namely, in the breakaway Abkhazia. During Soviet times, Georgia had no strong and independent industrial production, and even the few factories that managed to survive the painful first years of independence, such as the metallurgical, chemical, cement, and fertilizer plants, could not survive without the centralized economy and steady and uninterrupted supplies of raw materials. Even more so, much of its agricultural potential was devastated because of the conflict sparked in 1992 in Abkhazia.

To his credit, Shevardnadze was a very shrewd politician. Called by some ill-wishers, "fox with a split tail," Shevardnadze was an exemplary diplomat when it came to turning the most uncomfortable and failing situations to his benefit. In 1983, at the 200th anniversary of the unification with Russia, he made the following public comment for which he was reprimanded repeatedly by political rivals: "Georgia is called the country of the sun. But for us the true sun rose not in the east but in the north, in Russia—the sun of Lenin's ideas."[120] His pro-Russian attitude radically changed because of the conflicts in Abkhazia and South Ossetia, who were backed up politically and economically by Russia. The reversal of Georgia's political course culminated at the 2000 election campaign, when Shevardnadze promised to bring Georgia to the North Atlantic Treaty Organization (NATO) by the end of his presidential term.[121] To Shevardnadze's credit, Georgia started showing a slow but sure drift towards the West politically, with its membership in NATO Partnership for Peace (PfP) in 1994, and economically, by joining, as a transit land, the energy carriers' transportation projects from the Caspian Sea to the European markets. Nevertheless, his legacy is tarnished by unresolved conflicts, thousands of refugees, and absolute economic downfall, but, paradoxically, quite stable although stagnant domestic political environment fostered through overwhelming and chronic corruption.

The corruption in Georgia deserves separate mentioning here. This phenomenon had deeply reaching roots. It was imposed by the Russian tsarist apparatus starting from the 18th century and further perfected by the Soviet bureaucratic machine. Independence brought to Georgia another type of corruption, called "state capture" by Wheatley, when "the political elite uses the apparatus of the state to further its own private interests."[122] This highly institutionalized form of corrupt behavior was accepted by the larger masses of society with very little resentment.

It was only after 2000 that the new democratic forces started to appear in the Georgian establishment, which by 2003 consolidated around the triumvirate of the young Georgian politicians Mikheil Saakashvili, Zurab Zhvania, and Nino Burjanadze. Saakashvili, a U.S.-sponsored and educated lawyer who was practicing commercial law at Patterson, Belknap, Webb, and Tyler, joined the Parliament of Georgia in 1995. Soon after entry into the Georgian political scene, Saakashvili ignited the democratization processes modeled after the United States. These moves included the merit-based election of judges to the local courts, initiation of the prison reforms, and the anti-corruption campaign in the early-2000s. In November 2003, as a result of the Parliamentary elections called by the Organization for Security and Co-operation in Europe

(OSCE) a "spectacular fraud"[123] orchestrated by Shevardnadze's political circles, the progressive forces led by young triumvirate flooded the streets of Tbilisi and other major Georgian cities in what became known as the bloodless "Rose Revolution."[124] Saakashvili accused Shevardnadze of a massive manipulation of votes; his followers stormed Parliament, bringing democracy to Georgia with a single red rose.

Democratic transformations, however, were not endemic to Georgia, although it was born in the minds of the Georgian people tired of the inept and corrupt government unable to solve even the simplest problems of its population, such as ensuring 24/7 electricity and gas. The change was fostered and supported from outside. The United States has been the primary lobby state of Georgia ever since its independence, supporting it mostly financially. Linkoln Mitchell notes "that by 2003, the United States wanted Shevardnadze to move Georgia in a more democratic direction, with a special focus on parliamentary elections. . ."[125] According to a Congressional Research Service note, Georgia regularly led the list of world states in terms of per capita U.S. economic aid. Between 1992 and 2010, Georgia has received U.S.$3.3 billion. In 2001, the economic support was U.S.$87.1 million; another U.S.$87 million was earmarked for 2012, with a subsequent budgetary appropriation request for U.S.$68.7 million in 2013.[126] These means were directed in support of the Georgian democratic institutions, cultural heritage retention, economic development, and military aid.

As a result of titanic efforts to change the mentality and the culture of corruption and nepotism, the new government after the Rose Revolution undertook a number of significant steps to eradicate the culture of bribery and preferential treatments. This led to the dismissal of significant numbers of officials, a decade later many of whom joined in opposition to Saakashvili. Currently, Georgia is viewed by many as an exemplary young democracy with an effective rule of law and liberalized society, notwithstanding the unsuccessful war with Russia in 2008[127] and continuous domestic political havoc of the power diarchy between President Mikheil Saakashvili and the incumbent Prime Minister Bidzina Ivanishvili, an ethnic Georgian tycoon from Russia.

Independent Belarus.

The last years of the Soviet Union gave rise to nationalist feelings in Belarus. Suddenly the people started to realize that they are different from Russians, notwithstanding their strong linkages with Russia, including linguistic and cultural similarities, and the centuries-long acceptance of the fact that they are an inseparable part of the overall Russian ethnos.[128] The Belarus Popular Front was created in 1988, and, from the onset, started to prepare the country for the forthcoming independence. Already by the early-1990s, the Belarusian political establishment and the public felt strong winds of change. In 1990, while still within the USSR, Belarusian Supreme Soviet declared its state sovereignty without having de facto independence. Independence came a year later when, in December 1991, the heads of the three Slavic Soviet republics—Ukraine, Belarus, and Russia—concluded a historical agreement to dissolve the Soviet Union.

Similar to Georgia and Ukraine, in the first years of independence, Belarus was ruled by former communist party leaders: Stanislav Shushkevich as the chair of the Supreme Committee and Vyachaslav Kebich as the prime minister. However, neither of them lasted long; Shushkevich resigned under the burden of corruption accusations by Lukashenka, and Kebich lost the presidential elections to Lukashenka, who was rapidly gaining popular support. Lukashenka's ascent to power started from his membership in the Supreme Soviet in 1990, where he served as the chair of the Anti-Corruption Commission. Right from this time, Lukashenka revealed a craving for power via highly populist means. As the commission chair, Lukashenka did his best to show the people that he was a true leader. According to Savchenko:

> He exhibited all the conspicuous stringency of a common man visibly outraged by the machinations of nefarious elites, promptly accusing top officials, including . . . Kebich and . . . Shushkevich of embezzlement, abuse of office, and general corruption.[129]

By the majority of indicators, Belarus is the most autocratic out of the three countries in this analysis. Its current president, Lukashenka, has been ruling the country with an iron fist ever since 1994. Immediately after the elections, Lukashenka applied heavy-handed authoritarian tactics aimed at staying *vser'ez i nadolgo*—"for real and for long."[130] After the elections, Lukashenka undertook a number of steps directed towards limiting the fundamental freedoms of its own citizens, including the freedom of speech. He "censored state media, closed Belarus' only independent radio station and several independent newspapers . . ."; ignored the decisions of the Supreme Court proclaiming his decrees as unconstitutional; blocked the impeachment claims by the opposition by organizing the popular referendum in 1996, granting the power to rule over the parliament, eventually disbanding it with the Russian support; and establishing a fully puppet legislator.[131] According to Juri Cavusau, between 2003 and 2005, Lukashenka's government shut down 347 NGOs,[132] while most of the remaining ones were forced to go underground or to immigrate to the Baltic States, such as the Belarusian Institute for Strategic Studies, the leader in independent policy analysis. The limitations of civil society activities were institutionalized in the form of Article 193 of the Belarusian Criminal Code, which envisages 2 years in prison for cooperation with unregistered NGOs, while Article 293 holds punishments for those who train people involved in public protests.

Systematic gross human rights violations, suppression of political freedoms and rights of its citizens, and persecutions of the political opposition became the distinctive feature of Lukashenka's autocratic regime. The recent establishment of an ideological expertise office within the Ministry of Defense over the public administration's decisions[133] further strengthens the positions of the "last dictator in Europe." The following description of Lukashenka's character by Brian Bennett tells a lot about this long-lasting leader with personality cult:

> Lukashenka was a loner. He saw no need to belong to a political party. . . . He was uniquely fitted to rolling up his sleeves and making decisions without sharing the burden or delegating. He liked the idea of the presidential system: it offered the prospect of power without having to cooperate much with others or make promises. Sharing power did not suit his temperament.[134]

Petr Kravchenko, former Minister of Foreign Affairs of Belarus, gave another very vivid account of Lukashenka's character:

> like a 16-year-old youth wants intimacy with a woman, so Lukashenka with any fiber of his spirit, every cell of his organism, desired power as such. Because power for him was the real pleasure, in a way, as an end in itself and as a pleasure in wealth.[135]

The thirst for power of a typical Soviet-style apparatchik personality of Lukashenka at the dawn of his career became the trademark of the future autocrat.

Economically, Belarus did not "get out" of the Soviet Union in complete shambles, unlike Georgia. The country kept most of its industrial potential intact and working, including oil refineries processing Russian oil and transiting it further to Europe; valuable natural resources processing, such as the potash mines, metallurgical, and chemical plants; and heavy industrial equipment factories, such as the Soviet giant MAZ truck factory and MZKT which manufactures heavy military machinery. These industrial capabilities, together with most of the economic potential of the country, are currently controlled by Lukashenka and his loyal oligarchs.

Belarus is no stranger to foreign aid, although not on the scale of Ukraine and Georgia. The assistance was provided mostly in the form of developmental grants to the Belarusian civil society from Western democracies. The United States has been supporting democratic institutionalization for a number of years, although not encouraging the American companies to invest in Belarus due to overwhelming corruption and massive human rights violations. From 1992 through 2007, total U.S. assistance to Belarus amounted to

U.S.$340.96 million, with an additional U.S.$141.36 million in the form of the Freedom Support Act with the assistance apex in 1993 reaching U.S.$129.87 million (little less than half of all assistance) and dropping dramatically with Lukashenka's ascent to power, with the lowest point in 2007 of U.S.$0.15 million.[136] Economic aid is closely followed by sanctions, including visa restrictions for Lukashenka, his closest entourage, and corrupt businesses and firms.[137] The EU also tried to help Belarus; in 2011-13, the EU assistance programs of the European Commission amounted to €17.3 million.[138] Finally, individual European governments, including Belarus' immediate neighbor, Poland, extended their support, which, according to Gordon Fairclough, amounted to U.S.$120 million in aid to opposition groups.[139]

CAN DEMOCRACY LEAD TO POLITICAL STABILITY?

The data on the levels of democracy, political stability, and economic development, as well as the public perceptions of these variables in Ukraine, Georgia, and Belarus presented earlier, differ significantly with respect to their post-independence performance. All three countries jumpstarted their histories anew after 1991 and, at first glance, should have taken similar paths considering vast similarities in their pre-independence state and general social cultural resemblance. However, as the countries progressed further into an independent existence, they evolved in completely different directions.

A significantly high corruption level and unsatisfactory human rights conditions in Ukraine fit within its comparatively low political stability. Georgia is characterized by vibrant democracy, coupled with a low level of political stability alongside its poor economic performance. It is ahead of Ukraine and Belarus with its low corruption measures and relatively better situation with the human rights. The lowest democratic indicators in Belarus are intertwined with the highest level of political stability among all three countries, as well as good economic and social conditions created by the authoritarian governance for its people. The causes of the governance puzzle are deeply rooted in the diversity of the political cultures of Georgia, Ukraine, and Belarus and how they respond to globalized democratization.

Ukraine.

Ukraine is politically, economically, and culturally fragmented with several powerful centers of gravity. The rivalry between these poles creates an uneasy domestic environment that negatively affects political stability and economic development. Relationship between these variables has been unstable ever since its own Orange Revolution. Post-revolutionary disillusionment is quite frequent in politically volatile countries. Desperate electorates usually put too much hope in their leaders, who tend to over-promise their supporters, hoping for favorable votes. In Ukraine, on top of its political fickleness, the society rushed from one extreme to the other. A historically preexisting geographic divide was exacerbated by political diversity of the regional actors, with Yushchenko representing mostly the west and central Ukraine and Yanukovych harnessing his support from the pro-Russian East.

The process that led to the Orange Revolution started as a response to the political stalemate of

Kuchma's government. The most important choice for the country, which, according to Krushnelnycky, was "wedged between the European Union and an increasingly autocratic Russia"[140] was born out of the quest for the modern Ukrainian identity, on the one hand; and the popular repulsion of omnipresent corruption, chronic electoral fraud at all levels, the old Soviet style of governance, and overwhelming power centralization, on the other. After the fiasco with the fulfillment of the Orange Revolution pledges, political regionalization exacerbated. The pro-Western and pro-Russian forces did not lose their political orientations, but, under the changing realities, this was no longer a matter of concern. The south part of Ukraine is quite a special case, which is somewhat centrist and balanced. According to the Razumkov Center's poll, only 1.3 percent of the sample of respondents believed that Yushchenko's government had fulfilled its election promises.[141] The post-revolutionary apathy and overall disappointment with the incompetence of Yushchenko's government to solve the vital problems of economic and social development of the country led to a comeback of the Orange Revolution underdog, Yanukovych, first as prime minister in 2006 and later, in 2010, as president.

Under the current circumstances, political stability is understood in Ukraine as the peaceful dialogue and political consensus between the opposition and the government. Ideally, the process of political communication between various political factions can be safeguarded by strong democratic institutions, such as parliament, making viable decisions and supervising their fulfillment. Due to the highly volatile domestic content before and immediately after the Orange Revolution, the Ukrainian political establishment is looking for a high predictability of governance. One possible explanation for this is that the political environment in Ukraine, especially after the failure of the results of the revolution to live through the next elections, had become more insensitive, more thick-skinned to withstand the influences of the political processes. There is, however, an important difference between political predictability and political stability. While in both cases the political environment is shielded from internal and external disturbances, political stability offers the continuity of political processes, whereas political predictability offers the ability to predict political processes via institutional mechanisms of power retention; all other instances of hypothetical political change connote political unpredictability.

From the point of view of internal political stability, the current situation in Ukraine is mostly immune from large-scale and unexpected transformation. This is achieved by high quasi-authoritarian resilience of the government, which, nevertheless, allows for some expressions of political deviance, unlike in Belarus. There is no catastrophic political or economic crisis, but the disillusionment of society is total after the disastrous outcomes of the revolution and their apathy for any repeated tries to change reality. The logic "we tried; it did not work; why bother again?" is overwhelming among the domestic polity. This is notwithstanding (or, perhaps, due to) the fact that the political sphere, the state apparatus, the judiciary, and the political parties are considered the most corrupt institutions in Ukraine.[142] There are many in Ukrainian society willing to give up some of their freedoms to keep the country away from political instability, which negatively affects their economic well-being.

At the same time, due to high political regionalization, the prospects for peaceful transition of power
are quite vague. A domestic elitist environment is
highly polarized, but paradoxically, interrelated and
presents multiple forces of power each with its own
agendas and lobbies.

The human rights situation remains within the focus of many external actors, including human rights
watchdogs and international organizations. The most
conspicuous case is the ongoing imprisonment of
Yulia Tymoshenko, former prime minister and current opposition leader. Her "alleged ill-treatment in
prison where she is serving a 7-year sentence, and
two of her former political allies,"[143] raises the concerns of the EU and the United States. According to
Freedom House:

> Ukraine suffered a decline for a second year due to
> the politically motivated imprisonment of opposi-
> tion leaders, flawed legislative elections, and a new
> law favoring the Russian-speaking portion of the
> population.[144]

Tymoshenko still has her supporters who are not numerous but, nevertheless, represent a political power
that cannot be neglected — over 18 percent of the vot-
ers support her party, *Bat'kivshina* (Fatherland).[145]

In Ukraine, internal political stability is not connected with the effectiveness of democratic institutions; it
depends more or less on a strong economic base and
absence of any significant political disturbances. Due
to the overwhelming political and economic control
of the current leadership, the chances for a forceful
change of the ruling regime in the Orange Revolution
style are quite limited, at least in the short run. Notwithstanding quite serious clashes between different

clans and power interest groups, there is a high level of political predictability of Yanukovych's "Party of Regions" not to yield its power to the opposition in any perceivable future. The government is highly resilient and monolithic with strong elites increasing family- and clan-based political fragmentation with the rest of the Ukrainian population.

The absence of real and tangible change after the Orange Revolution had somewhat discredited the forces presently in the opposition. Failure of the revolution stiffled a previously active Ukrainian civil society, putting it into a lethargic sleep. Advocates for political transformations attribute this tenacity of the government to the overall passivity of the public. On the other side of the political spectrum, there is also no common vision and consensus on how political change would happen among opposition forces, which are separated by their internal quarrels. The most recent development in the Ukrainian political arena is the decision of Vitaliy Klichko, the world boxing champion and chairman of the pro-Western party, Ukrainian Democratic Alliance for Reform (UDAR), to run for the forthcoming March 2015 presidential elections, while calling for the rest of opposition leaders to unite.[146] This, however, does not mean that the two remaining opposition candidates— Arseniy Yatsenyuk and Oleh Tyagnibok—will withdraw from the presidential race. The real opponent of Yanukovych, according to Victor Sumar, is neither of these candidates, but the dire "economic situation, social discontent, and numerous 'discriminated' businesses that can manage to support the opposition."[147]

The process of democratic institutionalization in Ukraine is still undergoing growing pains. Here, individual trust prevails over organizational trust. This trust is, however, not stable, which reflects the changing loyalties to individual institutions. A part of the fluctuating preferences is that actors have chameleon loyalties to different institutions and may very easily switch their preferences, leading to high political unpredictability. This makes the domestic political environment extremely volatile. A peculiar nature of Ukrainian political culture is extremely low popular understanding of democratic institutions and their purposes. To a certain extent, this is due to the organizational behavior of incumbent government: political revenge. Not only does each incoming power get rid of most of the representatives of the former ones, it also engages in political persecutions. The most notorious cases are the imprisonment of Tymoshenko in 2011 and Yuri Lutsenko, also the inspirer of the revolution and former Minister of Interior, in 2010 (pardoned in 2013); both were charged with corruption and embezzlement of public funds.

Absence of a clear correlation between democracy and economic development can be explained by skyrocketing corruption and elitist economies. From the point of view of economic development, there is little economic stability due to the elitist nature of the business transactions. Since the economy does not benefit everyone, the biggest problem here is that there is no well-developed and established middle class, which is the backbone of any democratic society. According to the Razumkov Center, there is the phenomenon of:

> Ukrainian middle class [which] is emerging as a 'new middle class' in the Western perception of the term—i.e., as the middle class whose social basis is made up by specialists (rather than owners).[148]

74

This means that the middle class is not self-sustainable in the long run and is very much project and program dependent. Among the factors impeding the flourishing of the middle class, the following can be mentioned: underestimated cost of labor, very high level of shadow social relations, and crisis of the state legal system. As a result, the authors of the article concluded:

> the middle class as the social backbone of civil society, not established yet, and the authorities of a state not ruled by law can be neither partners nor opponents, as they are estranged from each other and never meet, existing 'in parallel worlds'.[149]

In addition to the uncertainty within the opposition ranks and the popular apathy, the government is also at a political limbo with regards to its foreign political course. External political stability of Ukraine depends on the balance between the two factors: the historical cultural, political, and economic influence of Russia, and the craving of Ukraine to join (return) to the family of European nations. The Russian factor has been both the positive and negative force in domestic Ukrainian politics, pressing on it politically and economically whenever it showed signs of drifting away from its geopolitical space. Russia traditionally has been one of the largest foreign investors in the economy of Ukraine, both by the amount of FDIs[150] as well as other, less transparent investments. According to Boris Heifetz:

> Russian business owns in Ukraine four out of six oil refineries, almost all non-ferrous metallurgy plants; has its interests in the energy sector, steel industry and began expansion in engineering, chemical industry, and the financial sector.[151]

However, the money is invested not to contribute to economic development, but the contrary—to hinder it. A vivid example includes the shipyard Zarya in the Crimea, which was bought by the Russian United Shipyard Company, and its production is steadily decreasing not to present competition to Russian shipyards.[152]

The other foreign policy direction is towards the West and, more specifically, Europe. This part of Ukrainian identity is, however, quite weak. According to a public opinion poll conducted by the Razumkov Center, Ukraine is considered a European country only historically and geographically—by other parameters, including economically, socially, politically, and culturally, the sample respondents considered Ukraine as a non-European country.[153] Moreover, only 12.3 percent of the respondents consider themselves Europeans.[154] Ukraine is a part of the European Neighborhood Initiative (ENP) and the Eastern Partnership (EaP). It has a separate Partnership and Cooperation Agreement (PCA) with the EU to foster further integration. Ukraine is about to sign the next important milestone, the Associated Agreement with the EU, which will harmonize its economic, political, and cultural basis with the latter.

The Ukrainian government is trying to keep the visibility of balanced policy, showing clear aspirations towards ultimate membership in the EU but, at the same time, signing the Memorandum on the Observer Status in the Customs Union with Russia.[155] On the one hand, this is a nonexistent status in a nonexistent entity, which brings no tangible benefits to Ukraine, even in the long run. On the other, however, with this step, Ukraine pledged not to undertake the steps that could harm the Customs Union, which is directly against the Euro-integration process, which, on its own account, is quite sluggish. For its part, Russia does not refrain from using the economic tools of its soft-power pressure on Ukraine to keep it within its own spheres of influence. An example of such economic blackmail is the recent ban imposed on all Ukrainian imports to Russia.[156]

Another part of the external political stability is covered by the NATO factor. Mykola Sungurovskiy noted several obstacles to the successful Euro-Atlantic integration of Ukraine:

> [a]bsence of national consensus and consolidation of political forces and society; lack of political will and strategic management at the level of state administration [and] the influence of the 'Russian factor'.[157]

Even after the Soviet Union, NATO remains the major security threat for many in the eastern parts of the country. According to one of the public opinion polls, most Ukrainians (61.9 percent) do not support NATO enlargement,[158] and this number is traditionally higher in the Eastern regions under the predominant Russian political, cultural, and economic influence. Another 44.5 percent of respondents think that Ukraine should abandon its plans to join NATO,[159] and numbers of those who would not support Ukraine's accession to NATO has always been very high.[160]

Inability of current Ukrainian government to choose a foreign policy course and strictly adhere to it (due to multiple reasons) shows the political dualism inherent to the Ukrainian political culture. According to Pavel Haydutski, in Ukraine:

[s]ome give priority to the European vector, others—Eurasian. However, all [are] trying to appeal to the public's opinion and manipulate them. Today, in addition to studying public opinion on this matter, the legal mechanisms—the referendum—can be enacted. As a result, Ukraine, in fact, moved even closer to the danger of the split society.[161]

The "identity split and confusion of values"[162] is also mentioned by Mikola Riabchuk in his analysis of the Ukrainian political future.

Under the current political realities of weak and segmented opposition, a strong grip on power of the current leadership and political lethargy of the masses, the domestic political climate is notable for its high predictability, at least for the short run. Notwithstanding some internal friction between various interest groups and oligarchs within the ruling regime, domestic political landscape has some degree of stability. Under the contemporary Ukrainian realities, political stability is achieved by means of an intractable government not conducive to political change, which is very close to the definition of political stability used here. At the same time, there are some signs of the "Party of Regions" losing control over Kyiv and other central areas. The future of the retention of power within the close cycles of the "Party of the Regions" is through keeping Yanukovych in power for another term or coming up with his approved successor for the subsequent elections round. With all the growing popular discontent among the politically active population, the propensity for the Ukrainian political establishment to witness its own version of Lukashenka is quite low.

Georgia.

The real test for democracy happened in Georgia in October 2012. The United National Movement (UNM) party under President Saakashvili lost the parliamentary elections to its main contender, the "Georgian Dream," headed by billionaire Bidzina Ivanishvili, who made most of his fortune in Russia. By publicly acknowledging the defeat during the parliamentary elections, Saakashvili's government showed high "democratic resilience." According to a Human Rights Watch report, the elections "marked Georgia's first peaceful transition of power since independence,"[163] which is a significant achievement in this turbulent country, especially after the painful defeat in the war against Russia in August 2008.

Freedom in the World 2013 mentioned Georgia as the "most notable positive political development in Eurasia" but also pointed out the post-election political persecutions of the opposition:

> Georgia, which experienced its first orderly transfer of power to the opposition through democratic elections, finished the year on a less than satisfying note after the new government quickly arrested some 30 officials of the previous government, raising concerns about politically motivated prosecutions.[164]

The Georgian opposition throughout the years has been known for having maximalist agendas. Since the early days of independence, the opposition has been trying not only to mend the shortcomings of the former governments, but also to destroy completely its achievements. Saakashvili's reign was remarkable for epic anti-corruption trials and prosecution of former government officials, with eventual dismantling of

Shevardnadze's "Citizens' Union" party. Ivanishvili's current government continues this line of politically motivated revenge by imprisoning former government figures, the most notable including the ex-Minister of Interior Kakha Targamadze, who was considered for a while as the front-runner for Saakashvili's party in the October 2013 presidential elections.

The notion of political stability is understood in Georgia as the predictability of future political development and the political continuity of powers. This means both the stability of a single political power within the constitutionally allowed framework and the anticipatory nature of governance, as well as the general sustainability of political environment as a whole. Georgia is on the path towards democratic institutionalization, which is more conducive to long-term political change, at least allowing for short-term political disturbances. Institutions as "systems of established and prevalent social rules that structure social interactions"[165] set the "humanly devised constraints that structure political, economic, and social interactions"[166] for their actors. In terms of democratic institutionalization, these tasks are achieved by the fully functioning, transparent, and fully accountable government apparatus, decreasing the propensity for the unstructured and/or forceful changes of governments and governances, and allowing for long-term political, cultural, and economic projects under the politically stable domestic climate.

In Georgian realities, the mere existence of democratic institutions stipulated the presence of democracy. Having been a victim of multiple internal and external disturbances, there is an overwhelming consensus among Georgian society to avoid political extremes by prognosis of forecasting future political changes. In a February 2012 survey conducted jointly by the National Democratic Institute and the Caucasian Research Resource Center, the views on whether Georgia was a democracy or not were equally split between the respondents.[167] From the point of internal political stability, considerable political maturity and political tolerance is required in order to provide for the fulfillment of democratic institutions. Instead, Georgia has been suffering for decades from political ambivalence. In a country where the political preferences of the electorate change with oscillating pendulum frequency, a political environment is stable only when it is based on a number of parameters. These parameters include a sustainable legal system protecting individuals and businesses from organized crime; a continuity of economic development through diversified business models; and protection of fundamental human rights and freedoms, including the freedom of opposition from political persecutions, is upheld. All these mean a developing political culture, i.e., the behavior of the actors within the legal institutional frameworks, which presupposes no frivolous interpretation of the institutional constraints.

Political stability in Georgia requires the presence of multiple political powers, which would create a healthy political competition with respect to the rules of engagement. Absence of these forces is, perhaps, one of the most important reasons for the low level of long-term political stability. There is no visible middle class to support democratic institutions. This point is very much in line with Lundell's argument on economic development being the precondition for democratization.[168] A well-established and vibrant middle class would further lead to sustainable and planned long-term political change since it would be more cautious to keep stability rather than biannual dramatic transformations. Long-term change will occur when democratic institutions are trusted and their decisions respected on a countrywide scale.

Another peculiarity in Georgian politics is high individual versus low institutional trust. Because the new government has just started, at this point in time, it enjoys high trust from the electorate willing to allow it some time for political try-outs. According to the National Democratic Institute (NDI) public opinion poll conducted in March 2013, Bidzina Ivanishvili enjoys the highest trust of the people, alongside the head of the Georgian Church (75 percent and 92 percent, respectively), while the trust in Saakashvili is three times less (25 percent). Ivanishvili's party also has more than 65 percent of trust of the Georgian population to solve vital issues, such as relations with Russia, economic development, healthcare, and law and order.[169] This can be temporary, however, depending on the actual performance of the new institutional actors.

On the other hand, institutional trust in Georgia, while being low, is quite selective. The domestic polity believes in its institutions on the basis of their individual performance. According to the Freedom House issue of *Nations in Transit 2012:*

> Confidence in the court system is slowly improving with 53 percent of respondents trusting the system in 2011 compared to 22 percent in 2007. Courts are better equipped and funded and generally perceived as less corrupt.[170]

The existing political diarchy between Saakashvili and Ivanishvili, however, tears the political blanket in the country in futile attempts to draw and retain the choices of the electorate. The October 2013 presidential elections mark an important milestone in the Georgian political history; they will show whether the country is ready for true democratic transformations.

External political stability in Georgia is intimately linked with the restoration of its territorial integrity. There is common consensus that, until the areas of Abkhazia and South Ossetia are back under Georgian jurisdiction, the country will continue to experience phantom threats to its political stability from Russia. External stability, in the view of many Georgians, consists of three hypothetical parts: return of the secessionist territories; membership of the country in NATO; and a balanced foreign policy, which places Georgia firmly among the interests of the major regional players, Russia and the EU included.

The first two parts of external stability are interchangeable and equally unattainable, at least in the perceivable future. If Georgia joins NATO, this would mean automatic inaction of the "one-for-all-and-all-for-one" Article 5 of the North Atlantic Treaty. This would inevitably draw the Alliance into political and possible military confrontation with Russia. The Greece-Turkey scenario over Cyprus would not be applicable here since Russia's membership in NATO is far more unrealistic than that of Georgia. NATO tries to avoid this political and military gambit with Russia but simultaneously sends promising but misleading messages to Georgia. NATO's General Secretary Anders Rasmussen recently said:

> [L]et me be clear. Meeting the requirements for NATO membership [for Georgia] must not be viewed only through a military prism. . . . As I look up the path ahead, I can see our shared destination of a stable and democratic Georgia at the heart of the Euro-Atlantic community. Georgia will become a member of NATO.

But further work is needed to meet the requirements of membership.[171]

This is one among many encouraging verbiages NATO has been sending for years to Georgian leadership.

In addition to its military nature, NATO has the mandate to support the democratization processes happening in the associated countries. Georgia is a member of the PfP program; it is involved in the Planning and Review Process (PARP) and has the Individual Partnership Action Plan (IPAP) for NATO membership. Georgia has repeatedly "declared NATO membership aspirations"; it has fully participated in NATO-led International Security Assistance Force (ISAF) in Afghanistan and the Operation ACTIVE ENDEAVOR in the Mediterranean. Finally, there is a special NATO-Georgia Commission to oversee the possible accession process. On the other hand, NATO has to understand that Georgian membership will bring it back in confrontation with Russia, who views Georgia and, largely Caucasus, as its *arrière-cour*, and NATO as its chronic nemesis.

The last part of the external stability — a balanced foreign policy — is also quite difficult to achieve. Georgian partnership with the EU is framed by a number of legal instruments, such as the Partnership and Cooperation Agreement (1999) and the European Neighborhood Policy Action Plan. It is involved in the negotiations over the association with the EU, including the Deep and Comprehensive Free Trade Agreement,[172] although much will depend on the will of the Georgian leadership. Being less under the direct pressure from the EU's main competitor than Ukraine and Russia, Georgia can freely advance on the path towards fuller integration with the EU, provided there is high commitment of the current government.

Finally, the discrepancy between a high level of democracy and low levels of political stability and economic development, which goes contrary to the "democratization hypothesis," can be explained by incongruence between form and contents of democratic institutions. Immediately after independence, Georgia took the path towards building democratic governance with its standard attributes, such as separation of the branches of power, free and transparent judiciary, law and order organizations, including the Ombudsman's office, and their relevant agencies. These institutions proposed by Western organizations, including the U.S. Government and the EU, as a means of democratic revival of the post-Soviet nations from communism, found a very receptive environment in Georgia. However, their contextual side—the essence of democratic institutions—has been lagging behind its formative part.

Belarus.

Belarus is a communism incarnate, with most of its spirit and letter, including the notorious abbreviation "KGB," a watchdog of state security. The Soviet Union has not lost its relevance for the contemporary Belarusian political environment. According to Balazs Jarabik and Alastair Rabagliati:

> Lukashenka exploited the nostalgia many Belarusians felt for the Soviet Union over a long period of time, although in reality he was busy building a new system of power, one which is different, both institutionally and functionally, from the Soviet model.[173]

Once in power, Lukashenka cut down all possible forms of a free country while leaving the domestic political landscape deprived of its early aspirations for a democratic state. The human rights violations became an inherent part of the system of governance in Belarus. *World Report 2013* informs:

> The government severely restricts freedom of expression. Most media is state-controlled, and television, radio, and internet censorship is widespread. Authorities continue to harass independent journalists for their work, including through arbitrary arrests, warnings, and criminal convictions. Journalists face great difficulties obtaining accreditation.[174]

As a matter of political control over the opposition, Wilson mentions the existence of secret "death squads" operating in Belarus since the late-1990s.[175]

Notwithstanding mostly repressive tactics, the domestic political environment was not always cloudless for Lukashenka. Time and again, protesters appear united in the common aspiration to ignite regime change. These opposition actors were, however, quickly suppressed, with subsequent harassment of the general population to prevent the expressions of disagreement. The failed "Jeans Revolution" in 2006,[176] an analogy with the revolutions in Georgia and Ukraine, was a response to the rigged presidential elections leading to suppression of the opposition and imprisonment of its leader, Alexander Kozulin, with charges of "hooliganism and incitement to mass disorder."[177] The public rallies were repeated during the 2010 presidential elections, when about 700 protesters, among them seven presidential candidates, were sentenced with similar charges. Some of them, including presidential candidate Andrei Sannikov, sustained serious bodily injuries.[178] The websites of opposition parties and groups were hacked and taken down, and their leaders thrown in jail.[179] According to the *Independent's* report, Lukashenka's "security forces have gone after his opponents with a ferocity that would not have looked out of place in Soviet times."[180] Another cycle of protests hit Belarus in 2011, with thousands of people demanding Lukashenka's resignation.[181] As a result, the regime outlawed further assemblies and public gatherings.

Political stability has its peculiarities in Belarus. The authoritarian resilience keeps all the political processes under its strict control, which diminishes the propensity for popular upheaval. The current high level of stability in Belarus is explained by growing internal contradictions in the economic and political structures. Vertical authoritarian model copes well with standard situations of domestic shocks and is largely immune to external challenges, too, but is not very capable of evolving and solving crises. Economic shocks extrinsic to the political system (global crisis of 2009 and the domestic crisis of 2011) require responses in the form of modernization and reform, but they can undermine the foundation of the most authoritarian systems. In other words, a systemic change is required, but the system is not used to such changes. In essence, the notion of "political stability" can be applied to the vitality of Lukashenka's regime per se and not the ability of the country to survive the external and internal shocks. Belarus is among those consolidated authoritarian regimes, especially with a high degree of legitimacy (but not legality), which quite naturally would show "better" results from political and economic standpoints than the number of liberal democracies.

Political stability in Belarus, thus, depends on two factors: the autocratic leadership of Lukashenka (internally) and Russian economic subsidies (externally). The internal stability is explained by the iron-fist politics of Lukashenka, who created one "of the world's most repressive states,"[182] and with its systematic human rights violations and stifling of the freedoms of the Belarusians, which dissuaded them from any expressions of free will. The Belarusian paradox is in legitimizing the governance regime — "fitting" it within the polity — by the high level of authoritarian leadership of a single autocrat, by suppressing the civil and political freedoms and liberties, and by allowing for the development of socio-economic parameters of the country. This paradox, at first glance, refutes the thesis on the middle class being the backbone for democracy. Unlike most of the countries where the middle class prefers to keep democratic governance because it would allow it to have a better future via protecting their freedoms and economic interests, in Belarus the middle class is credibly harassed by Lukashenka to a point where it prefers to keep the situation as it is in fear that it could get worse.

An overview of the study, "Social Situation in Belarus in 2009," conducted by the Belarus Institute of Strategic Studies,[183] gives a good picture of the total political and economic stagnation in the country. Most of its respondents (39.5 percent) do not anticipate any changes in their economic well-being and 54 percent do not worry about losing their jobs in coming years. Of the respondents, 58.9 percent believe that nothing has changed in the state's support in times of economic crisis; 46 percent are satisfied with what the government does with varying degrees of problems. Out of those who are not happy with the government, 37.9

percent do not think that anything can be changed, and 48.8 percent do not think that public uprising is possible due to the worsening of the economic situation, whereas 52.4 percent absolutely deny their participation in the riots and demonstrations. A total of 54.8 percent do not want to go on strike; 44.5 percent will not sign any petition or appeal to the government; 47.5 percent will not help the families of the protesters; and 67.0 percent will not participate in any forceful actions against their government. At the same time, 48.4 percent do not plan to immigrate, of which 26.9 percent do not want to leave because they are happy with what they have.

Given a relatively high degree of forced legitimacy of the political regime and despite the repeatedly rigged elections at all levels, the weakness of the political opposition and dissent in society, and the apparent cohesion of the ruling elite, the stability of the current political regime appears to be high. By a systematic policy of repressions, Lukashenka dissuaded any political activity that deviates from his approved course. The Human Rights Watch states that currently "[a]t least 12 political prisoners remain jailed. Allegations of torture and mistreatment in custody persist."[184] According to the study conducted by the Independent Institute of Socio-Economic and Political Research, the predominant number of respondents (60.7 percent) believe that everybody is afraid to express their political views. With that, most of the respondents (51.1 percent) consider that human rights are provided; 68.1 percent claimed that the government did not abuse their rights; and only 26 percent think that their rights were violated.[185] The resulting stagnation in political thought is overwhelming and omnipresent in the daily lives of people and in the country's economy, where the government-based racket stifles small and medium businesses.

Among the positive traits of the current regime is the coverage of the primary needs of the population, which, on the one hand, discourages ordinary citizens from taking political actions in protection of their rights. This is the clear case where economic benefits significantly overweigh political ones. According to another study of the same think tank, most people (42 percent) view an ideal country as the one in which they can be successful and make good money. Similarly, on the question, "What would you do if you were the president in a country with hardships and unhappy people?" 41.6 percent answered that they would create the conditions where citizens could be successful and make good money,[186] while 72 percent of the respondents consider themselves supportive of the current government.[187]

Belarusian developmental authoritarianism is based on a comparatively better economic and social situation and on the control over larger industries and businesses by the close circle of elites. The *Index of Democracy 2011* notes:

> rampant corruption, small elites control the bulk of their nations' assets, institutions have been corroded by the effects of minerals-based development (the Belarusian regime depends on Russian subsidies), and governance and social provision are poor.[188]

All these became possible by the:

> state control over the economy [which] allowed President Lukashenka to starve opponents of resources and black-knight support from Russia [which] limited the regime's vulnerability to Western democratizing pressure.[189]

Belarusian elites are under Lukashenka's absolute control and enjoy his somewhat patrimonial approach and the divide-and-rule policy which prevents them from being too independent. As Alexander Feduta claims, Lukashenka, being the sole ruler of Belarus, did not consider it wise to steal from himself. He viewed "the whole country as his household, and a good boss of the household, which Lukashenka considers himself to be, does not steal his own stuff."[190]

Due to the close nature of the Belarusian businesses to external oversight, the full extent of corruption is unknown. Some information on the shadow deals and the political persecutions in Belarus, nevertheless, sporadically appears mostly in the Russian press, when its Russian patrons are upset with Lukashenka's performance. This was the case with the information about the corruption and political pressure, as well as on Lukashenka's lavish lifestyle and the shadow gains of his pocket oligarchs.[191] The same was true with the movie that was supposedly a political blockbuster in Russia, *Godfather*, in which the pro-governmental Russian TV station NTV talked about mysterious disappearances and assassinations of political opponents to the regime and also quoting Lukashenka's statements on Hitler's regime being a model for his own governance.[192] Interestingly enough, the movie was made in 2010, and the events it covers go back to 1999; this shows the level of political manipulations and control between the two "brotherly" nations. In return, the Belarusian state channel ONT had a special program, which criticized Putin's propaganda drive in a Russian car and openly calling him "a fool on the road"[193] in reference to his test-driving a new Lada.

Despite these occasional mutual stings, Russia, for the most part, has been the biggest actor contributing to political stability of Lukashenka's regime and accounting for its highest level of economic development among the three countries. In 2011, Russia had more than 75 percent of the FDIs in the economy of Belarus.[194] In 2012, the FDIs decreased by almost a quarter,[195] but, nevertheless, the share of Russia was the highest: 46.7 percent.[196] For example, in 2009, Russia invested U.S.$4 billion in the Belarusian economy.[197] In 2011, Belarus became the sixth-most attractive foreign investment location for the Russian capital.[198] The politics and economy in Russian-Belarusian relations are entangled to a point when Lukashenka's domestic political support closely correlates with the fluctuation of Russian's financial backing. According to Margarita Balmaceda, the Russian oil giant "Lukoil supported Lukashenka's 2001 reelection campaign in exchange for promises that Naftan [the major Belarusian state-owned oil company] would be privatized. . . ."[199] So-called "rent relations" with Russia are used to support the government at a level sufficient to ensure the loyalty of the majority of the population. The Belarusian government can, thus, provide for a higher growth of welfare of its population (and, hence, a greater degree of forced legitimacy) than more democratic governments in other post-Soviet countries (including Ukraine and Belarus), which do not have such lavish and immediate external rents and try to foster economic development primarily through the implementation of structural long-term reforms.

Because of the systematic policy of eliminating political rivals, Lukashenka's governance faces no internal threats due to virtually absent systemic opposition and no external threats by too weak and unwilling external actors. The EU has lost active interest in Belarusian politics since freezing of the EU-Belarus Partnership and Cooperation Agreement in 1997. Currently, the EU pursues what it calls a "policy of critical engagement"[200] in Belarus through supporting the civil society development and imposing economic and travel sanctions on the country and its leadership.

These two factors—coercive legitimacy and external political "calm" achieved through autocratic resilience and support/inaction of the third parties, respectively—made the current system developed by Lukashenka quite stable. In the short-term, stability increased with deliberate restrictions imposed on the development of democracy based on a noncompetitive model of the public interest (corporatism). In the longer-term, various elites would inevitably grasp their interests, which under the conditions of the crisis of the personal model of stability (inevitable death of the leader whom the stability of the system is clinging on) can become destabilizing. In such a crisis situation, the main factor in the stability of the system can be the interference of external forces (mostly from Russia and less so the EU and the United States). The main question is whether the national institutions and, in particular, the ruling political elites will have enough time during the personal dictatorship to develop and fully perceive their interests via proposing acceptable successors.

POLITICAL CULTURE MATTERS

Three separate types of political behavior different from the communalistic ideology-infused political cultures started to develop in Ukraine, Georgia, and Belarus soon after their independence. While in all three cases, the process of defining their political egos happened through revival of historical roots, for the future identity constructs, the three nations had developed distinct political cultures. These political cultures — flexible (open and allowing change in Georgia), bifurcate (undetermined and ambiguous in Ukraine), and latent (dormant and suppressed in Belarus) — developed sets of preconditions affecting the democratic institutionalization and political stability in different ways.

The study of the three democratization projects received a dual correlation between their political cultures and the governance regimes. Not only does the political culture define the "fit" of the regime within the domestic polity (the citizens), but it also envisages the variations in the degrees of their durability. If the political culture is conducive to fluctuations, it will negatively affect the political stability, as it will be more open to the shifts within domestic polity and foreign influences than the political culture, which rejects change. In this latter case, political stability will be guaranteed by the regime type that predisposes specific behavioral patterns of its citizens.

Economic development also affects political stability. The more visible and affluent the middle class is, the more it would prefer internal and external stability. From the point of view of internal stability, accumulated wealth and property can be decreased as a result of sporadic and uncontrolled processes of unexpected political instability, such as revolutions, riots, civil unrest, and coup d'états. This can also happen during the short-term change of government within democratically accepted frameworks, such as impeachments of presidents or stepping down of the incumbent governments. Politically less active but better-off masses would prefer political alterations, hoping for the positive changes in their lives. Generally, a well-to-do electorate would prefer peace to war since it would have more to lose then to win from the participation of its country in military actions (given their uncertainty) and would also come up with increased unity in the face of negative political externalities.

Ukraine.

The evolution of Ukrainian political culture reflects the regional split between the West and the East. The roots for this conflicting bipolarity go back to the Brest Church Union in 1596, which divided the country into the Greek-Catholic (western) and Orthodox (eastern) regions. The signing of the Union and the subsequent religious schism led to a long and bloody struggle between the followers of the two Christian denominations in Ukraine and had far-reaching cultural consequences for the country as a whole. In modern times, almost all leaders of the country had the election slogans of closeness with Russia, giving the Russian language a status of second official state language, and with Russia's political, economic, and moral support. At the same time, they continue to seek integration with the western political structures in hopes of receiving economic support.

This was the case of Yushchenko and later Yanukovych, as well as all other political leaders of smaller scale. Political flirtation with the West by expressing the desire for integration with Western political structures, including the EU and NATO, resulted in simultaneous rejection of such moves by "removing Ukraine's aspirations to [NATO] membership from the list of the state policy priorities in the sphere of national security."[201] Such political oscillations turn to the detriment of the "other side" of the political orientation since Russia, too, demands political loyalty. As analyst Vadim Karasev, notes, "current Ukrainian-Russian relations are suffering from serious uncertainty, probably the biggest uncertainty for the entire period."[202] This was due to the fact that Ukraine has to make decisive steps in the nearest future in the direction of further integration with the EU, whereas Russia is pressing for Ukraine's membership in the Customs Union, the two conflicting prospects for its political, cultural, and economic future.

The Ukrainian political personality split suggests the general conceptualization of this phenomenon as the **Ukrainian predicament**, the core of its bifurcate political culture developed since the times of existence under the Polish-Lithuanian Commonwealth: to seek patrons abroad, instead of relying on the loyalty of local constituency. As it seems, for the purpose of attaining the domestic legitimacy, it is paradoxically transferred abroad to receive the legitimacy externally to prove it to the local constituencies. After having successfully risen to power, the leadership cannot abandon the *modus operandi* of playing on the two different boards and, eventually, both the external lobby-states and the domestic constituency become disillusioned in their political performance.

Another significant part of the political culture in Ukraine is popular apathy born as the result of the omnipresent electoral fraud and the inability to achieve high political impacts on the popular level. The orchestrated mass "protests," such as concerts or marches with paid participants holding banners of political parties they do not support, contribute to the public disillusionment of the potentially politically active citizenry and disbelief in their own ability to change things in the country. These facts stress the low levels of domestic legitimacy and efficiency of the governance and the self-destructive nature of current political culture, the political behavior, which is rather petty rent-seeking instead of being directed at attainment of long-lasting political capital and popular support.

Georgia.

The centuries of foreign dominance forced upon Georgia a political culture that is highly adaptive to fluctuations of the geo-political environments. A possible explanation of this phenomenon could be its geographic location, which put Georgia at the junctions and overlaps of the traditions and interests of the Western and Eastern hemispheres. Nevertheless, it is not easy to pinpoint what accounts for frequent modifications in Georgian political culture and what made the Georgian political establishments so conducive to new political realities. A possible explanation is in external environment: the Georgian nation, having been under constant threats of annihilation from numerous invaders, had to adapt its political behavior constantly to the influence of external factors in order to survive physically.

The existence of Georgia under Russian rule for more than 3 centuries is particularly notable from the point of view of the flexible identity of the Georgian political culture under the external influences. Ronald Suni very rightly pointed out the cultural change:

In the half-century of Russian annexation of Eastern Georgia . . . Transcaucasian society was irreversibly

transformed. The effects of the Georgian metamor-
phosis were fundamental and profound.... [W]ith the
Russian occupation, a historical progress began that
rent the fabric of traditional Georgian society, producing new opportunities and loyalties.... By the end of
the first 50 years of Russian rule, the once rebellious,
semi-independent dynasties of Georgia had been
transformed into the service gentry loyal to their new
monarch.[203]

This change turned to be quite durable: even after
a short period of its independence, Georgia, having
been annexed by the Soviet Union, forcefully or will-
fully, continued to follow its northern neighbor in the
political, cultural, and economic choices.

Another explanation for the pliable political culture is that Georgian society has been particularly
known for its cultural openness and the ability to easily accept, test, and live through the newly proposed
norms, be they cultural, economic, or political. The
process of norm socialization, "of inducting actors
into the norms and rules of a given community,"[204] has
always been easy for the Georgian establishment. A
good example of this is the changing orientation of the
Georgian elite after they had left the Turkish/Persian
sphere of influence and fell onto the Russian one. This
was revealed in the language selection, cultural as-
similation, and incorporation of external traits in their
everyday lives.

The current Georgian establishment follows the
path-dependence and the traditions of political ver-
satility of its former leadership, including Shevardnadze's political curtsy to Moscow on the sun rising
from the north for the Georgians; Zurab Zhvania's
statement at the Council of Europe meeting in 1999,
"I am Georgian and therefore I am European"; Saa-

kashvili's craving for the NATO membership for Georgia; and more recently, the carefully pro-Russian stance of the new Georgian leadership. These last developments in the political orientation in Georgia can be seen in purely cultural and economic acts, such as sending the Georgian athletes to take part in the Universiade Games in Russia in the summer of 2013, participation of Georgia in the 2014 Winter Olympic Games in Sochi, as well as talks on possible resumption of imports of the Georgian to Russia banned well before the war of 2008. At the same time, Ivanishvili's government made recently a serious political statement showing aspirations to join the Eurasian Union, a proposed political entity of selected former Soviet republics, including Russia, Belarus, Kazakhstan, Kyrgyzstan, and Tajikistan — together with its breakaway regions.[205] If taken, this step with all its grave consequences for the Georgian political orientation could possibly become the most significant departure from the 2 decade-old Georgian pro-Western political and cultural orientation.

Belarus.

Unlike Georgia and, to a certain degree, Ukraine, the political culture in Belarus is limited-elitist, coercive, patrimonial, and mostly geographically homogenous. There is no regional political divide in Belarus, nor is the identity split as in Ukraine. The Belarusian political identity is not flexible to easily respond to change, as it is Georgia. It is *quittist*,[206] as Wilson describes, which signifies the highest possible level of apathy among the three countries. Whereas the Ukrainians had a limited chance to try and test the *vox populi* in action, and the Georgians experienced its lasting effects after their respective revolution, Belarusians were never given such opportunity to enjoy the democratic freedoms due to the highly oppressive ruling regime almost immediately after their independence. The dormant and suppressed Belarusian political culture is clearly seen in such defeatist popular statements of the critics of democratization as "Belarus is not ready for democracy," which, as Alexei Pikulik contends, "are not just a way to secure ideological legitimization, but also a sincere belief of a significant part of the country's political class."[207] Here, too, unlike in Georgia and Ukraine, the polity prefers stagnant political stability to uncertain but vibrant change.

Another side of the political culture in Belarus is "limited-elitist" due to a lack of historically established interest groups and diverse elites who would engage in political interplay that would include potentially wider cycles of players. The benefits of the regime are provided to the small groups of individuals in or closely affiliated with the ruling circle. As a result of the highly paternalistic and feudal political culture developed under Lukashenka, the elites do not possess the real power to influence the domestic political environment. There are no significantly strong personalities or charismatic figures, let alone opposition leaders (not jailed), who would possess enough political gravitas to instigate cultural change among the electorate. The regime simply "buys the loyalty" of those groups who may be affected by economic liberalization, which is identified with democratization. This is evident on the level of external political stability, where large industrial enterprises and agricultural business are subsidized via lavish Russian donations. Russia supports the existing Belarusian political-economic model via direct grants and loans, "energy rebates," including in exchange for mostly symbolic military and political alliance with the former.

The political culture in Belarus is also "minimalist" in a sense that the domestic institutional actors prefer the token satisfaction of the primary needs in fear that "it could get worse." In comparison to the post-independence economic, social, and political chaos of most of the ex-Soviet republics, including the civil wars in Georgia and economic hardships in Ukraine, the people in Belarus choose to have minimal but guaranteed benefits offered by their government rather than try to change the situation in pursuit of vague benefits. These include the average quality but free medical services; local enterprises making mediocre profits but not "owned" by foreigners, which signifies the perceived pride in independence; state-owned enterprises offering more stability than private ones; and predominant popular preferences for lower wages, but with guaranteed jobs.[208] The minimalist political culture, according to Silitski, is:

> [a] replica of the old Soviet one, but at a lower level of incomes with the following common expression regarding democracy, 'We don't need this democracy with hullabaloo. We need a democracy when a person works, earns some wages to buy bread, milk, sour cream, sometimes a piece of meat to feed his baby'.[209]

Such a stance is well aligned with the preferences of the majority of the local polity for economic benefits as opposed to political freedoms.

DEMOCRATIZATION THROUGH "REGIME MIMICRY"

Most of the modern societies that had sprung up as a result of the imperial collapses, including the post-Soviet nations, do not try to reinvent the wheel. They all tend to adopt already existing and tested governance frameworks, which are mostly democratic. Their choice for the governance regimes is mainly based on two considerations. On the one hand, the new nations reveal purely rational anticipation of political and economic benefits concomitant upon joining the newly acquired hosts of like-minded but developmentally advanced nations. This is what James March and Johan Olsen call the "logic of expected consequences" when institutional actors make their choices in pursuit of increased anticipated utility. The other reason is contained in the wish to "look alike" with the rest of the democratic community of states by copying/pasting their democratic structures and institutions that had proved effective there and, thus, should, in principle, achieve the same success in the local political, economic, and cultural environments. Such a behavior is based on the "logic of appropriateness": the countries consider it suitable to adopt the norms, rule, and practices of the democratically advanced societies because this is how they start viewing themselves.[210] There can be, of course, the combination of both choices, and the variable of political culture is fundamental in understanding the rationales behind them since it defines the modes of responses of democratizing nations to external and internal institutional challenges.

The choice goes for democratic institutions as opposed to those of other regimes because, through its institutional mechanisms, it provides most of the political stability in the long run and creates more durable conditions for the economic development of the policy. The regimes created in Georgia and Ukraine fall under the category of "hybrid," which are not yet fully democratic but already not completely authoritarian (and the qualitative and quantitative data gathered here confirms that). In the year preceding the Rose Revolution, Lucan Way and Steven Levitsky placed Ukraine (Georgia was absent from the analysis) within the "competitive authoritarianism" subsection of the "hybrid regimes" since their:

> formal democratic institutions are widely viewed as the principal means of obtaining and exercising political authority. Incumbents violate those rules so often and to such an extent, however, that the regime fails to meet conventional minimum standards for democracy.[211]

In the same issue, Larry Diamond placed Georgia and Ukraine into the category "ambiguous regimes" because they had "the form of electoral democracy but fail to meet the substantive test, or do so only ambiguously."[212]

The essential peculiarity of "hybrid regimes" is that they would allow for a limited degree of democratic expression of political choices of their constituencies without proper democratic internalization. The regimes, such as in Kuchma's Ukraine and Shevardnadze's Georgia, allowed for comparatively higher degree of political freedom.[213] Fully authoritarian regimes, such as in Belarus, rule with an iron fist and prevent any possible expression of political will, thus are more politically stable. However, they, too, choose the democratic facades. There, the political stability depends directly on the physical well-being of an autocrat and the degree of effectiveness of public coercion. As soon as the authoritarian regimes allow for some signs of political competition, skillful "norm entrepreneurs," such as Yushchenko and Saakashvili and later Ivanishvili, start to appear on the political scene and attempt to change the situation.

Implementation of the three democratization scenarios in Ukraine, Georgia, and Belarus is based on the externally provided blueprints. The democratic institutional frameworks are transplanted into their domestic realities by means of **regime mimicry** — a comprehensive process of political, economic, cultural identity change. This process is similar to isomorphic mimicry in biology, where "one organism mimics another to gain an evolutionary advantage."[214] An example of isomorphic mimicry is a frog, *Lithodytes lineatus* (commonly known as *Sapito listado*), living in Pan-Amazonia. *Lithodytes* is a harmless creature that is often confused with a highly poisonous *Allobates femoralis*. During the process of physical evolution, *Lithodytes* had adopted the form of its poisonous look-alike without its poisonous content to avoid being eaten by other creatures. In biology, this phenomenon is given the following explanation, "individuals of a more palatable species (mimic) gain advantage by resembling members of another, less palatable species (the model)"[215] in order to evolve into a seemingly dangerous form (usually a predator) to attain increased protection from other predators, while retaining the nonmalevolent content.

The scholarship on organizational management and economic development extends the notion of mimicry to such actors as "key suppliers, resource and product consumers, regulatory agencies, and other organizations that produce similar services or products"[216] from more developed countries. Here, the "[o]rganisations can mimic other organisations without having evidence that mimicry would actually increase functional performance."[217] According to Lant Pritchett *et al.*:

> [O]rganizations adopt—'modern' or—'best practice' forms or notional policies even when these are not followed up by, or are even consistent with, actual functional performance in the context of a given organization's actual capability for policy implementation. Moreover, these carbon-copy organizations are then asked to perform tasks that are too complex and/or too burdensome, too soon.[218]

Furthermore, Paul DiMaggio and Walter Powell talk about several types of organizational isomorphism: **coercive isomorphism** (formal and informal pressure on domestic organizations by their external counterparts and by cultural expectations of own society); **mimetic isomorphism** (when domestic organizations vaguely see their functions, they adopt the forms of other organizations hoping that what works there would work at home); and **normative isomorphism** (when organizational actors blur the distinction between organizational commitment and professional allegiances).[219] The difference between isomorphic and organizational mimicry is that while the former renders a life-saving service to its actor, the latter, on the contrary, fails the actor: isomorphism helps the species to survive and the organizational mimicry offers an ineffective remedy to the organizations by focusing on the formative and not contextual sides of the matters.

In matters of public governance, both "hybrid" and "authoritarian regimes" opt for the democracy to survive in new and vastly unfamiliar settings of the institutional jungle into which they were plunged. The regime mimicry develops where the whole governance regime mimics the advanced democratic institutions and notionally reflects the externally implanted and not organically developed rules, norms, and practices. In the field of democratic institutionalization, the regime mimicry would mean adoption of comprehensive forms of institutions of democratic governance (courts and the legal system, in general; offices of Ombudsmen; systems of human rights protection; elections; local self-governance agencies, etc.) without the full "lifecycle" of their socialization. This usually happens when newly independent nations, after the painful process of gaining sovereignty, suddenly side with the institutions of other countries that have been developed in the process of cognitive evolution. These nations are faced with the painful normative conundrums of defining their developmental paths and, while making the choice towards democracy, adopt the institutions of more democratically developed countries without proper grasp of their purpose and content.

Countries engage in regime mimicry for a variety of reasons. They may adopt practices of the institutions foreign to their popular "fit" because they would expect to receive purely tangible benefits from "joining the club" of democratic countries. These benefits may include developmental milestones through increased socialization with the countries whose institutions are adopted, such as memberships in international organizations (for instance, in the World Trade Organization [WTO] or NATO) through implementing institutional reforms. In this case, the mimicking countries will follow the "logic of expected consequences." They may also mimic the existing structures and undertake the reforms because they started associating themselves with the advanced democratic countries they want to look like. Here the benefits may also be available, but they are not the primary rationale for the regime mimicry; it is the identity construct that matters in building associations with other regimes. Such a behavior follows the "logic of appropriateness."

For a case comparison, consider the EU's external conditionality as an example of the externally provided institutional frameworks. Frank Schimmelfennig and Ulrich Sedelmeier identify three models of acceptance of institutional learning: the **external incentives model**, which "follows the logic of consequences and is driven by the external rewards and sanctions"; the **social learning model**, which follows the logic of appropriateness and emphasizes identification with the institutional model and "the legitimacy of its rules as key conditions for rule adoption, rather than the provision of material incentives"; and the **lesson-drawing model**, in which states adopt the "rules because they judge them as effective remedies to inherently **domestic** needs and policy changes rather than out of consideration about the incentives."[220] In this process of institutional socialization, the EU conditionality policies, or the *acquis communautaire*, create rational choice or identity-based frameworks for the countries to adopt the relevant institutions.

There is a fundamental difference between organizational and regime mimicries. Because of the sector-specific nature of the former, duplication of the externally imposed designs without essential touch with the domestic political, economic, and cultural grounds leads to their ultimate failure due to the low level of their holistic socialization. The functional spillovers within and across organizational and functional areas are possible, of course, and they may succeed up to a certain point, as the neofunctionalist logic goes.[221] But unless they include "specific socialization mechanisms (strategic calculation, role playing, normative suasion),"[222] their area of application will be limited to the precise organizations and, even narrowly, to units within them.

The process of regime mimicry is a dangerous path: a developing country could be dragged into the vortex of mimicked settings and, furthermore, into state failure. According to Philipp Krause, a:

> [p]art of the reason fragile states are hopelessly stuck is precisely because they try to mimic the formal institutions of success, rather than figuring out the functions of statehood on their own.[223]

In order for the mimicry to be successful, it should fully and completely transcend the societal fibers and become an inherent part of the political cultures of the mimicking nations. Regime mimicry can, indeed, turn into full-scale cognitive socialization, and this is where its greatest paradox lies: the fuller the mimicry, the higher the chances for it to turn into full normative socialization that would eventually end the mimicry.

Full mimicry exacerbates all three types of institutional learning models, as defined by Schimmelfennig and Sedelmeier, the types of spillovers and socialization patterns, and leads to the proper development of the normative "lifecycle" of democratization, including norm emergence, norm cascading, and norm internalization. The success of the regime mimicry is largely based on the ability of the countries to open up for the institutional change and not only to accept the proposed structured but, most importantly, to try to adjust them to their own realities. This is the crucial point in effective institutional change: increased mimicry accepted by the political elites would lead to the mutually interchanging process of adaptation of the mimicry to the societal "fits" and even deeper societal transformations of those "fits" for the nations in question.

In the matter of democratic transformations following either of the two logics, the societies with the flexible political cultures adopt the proposed frameworks either because others do so and they want to resemble them, or they expect certain benefits from the process of change. The only difference is in durability of the change. In both cases, the adoption starts via mimicry since the host societies have no or limited prior experience of the proposed institutions — as was the case with Ukraine, Georgia, and Belarus. At this stage, all three intervening variables will step in: the specific political culture, the force of external persuasion, and the economic condition of the target countries being under the influence of the specific logics guiding the agents of change.

The ideal condition for a full mimicry is the simultaneous existence of all three variables. For a country to start copying the institutional designs, there should be high enough external pressure on the parts of external and internal agents of change. In other words, the:

> [i]nternational organizations, local policy makers, and private consultants [should] combine to enforce the presumption that the most advanced countries have already discovered the one best institutional blueprint for development and that its applicability transcends national cultures and circumstances.[224]

The political cultures of the recipient societies should be highly conducive to change. Finally, countries must be economically more or less stabile to sustain the institutional change, which, as a transformation process, is always costly. These variables should be under the influence of both logics—appropriateness and consequentiality. This means that the societies should be both willing to identify themselves with the democratic institutions and be individually interested in receiving tangible benefits from the regime mimicry.

Presence of these three factors will lead to full and successful regime mimicry. New norms would emerge that would further develop into stable behavioral patterns. Further along in the mimicry, the norms would start cascading—they would transcend through larger societal layers, allowing for the participation of the increased number of institutional actors. Finally, the essence of mimicry would gradually fade, and the democratic normative internationalization will take place. Here, the paradox of full mimicry means that acceptance of new external designs will eventually turn into the appearance of new contexts.

The mimicry will be partial and less successful if either one, or all, of the three factors are absent. When the external pressure is low, i.e., when the agents of change approach the process negligently and halfheartedly, institutional design transfer will stumble upon the multiple external constraints, including the agents' own budgets and their allocations for the institutional support, their organizational management constraints, and the election cycles, to name a few. If the domestic political cultures of the host societies are intractable, they will continue to reject the externally proposed institutional changes until this process stalls. When economies of the mimicking countries experience hardships, the regime mimicry might slow down at the norm socialization since the countries would not be able to support financially further reforms processes. Finally, when used separately by the host societies, the two logics would lead to skewed visions on the proposed change. The logic of expected consequences alone would signal the external actors that the host societies are not interested in a cognitive change and only have short-term mercantile expectations with the set-in-stone preferences. Similarly, the logic of appropriateness would alarm external actors who would assume that the "like identities" were too early to develop and are based on too shallow institutional grounds. It would indicate that without proper material constraints and interests, the host societies are internally too feeble and overly receptive to the proposed transformations and may easily change their preferences.

In sum, unenthusiastically proposed institutions, coupled with the rigidity of the recipient countries' political cultures without proper financial backing, together with the bifurcate approach to the behavioral logics, create only partial mimicry. This mimicry would allow for the first stage in the norm "lifecycle" — norm emergence — and would inhibit subsequent stages of institutional socialization through norm cascading and internationalization. The changes would remain a facade because they face the rigid political cultures and the unwillingness of the regime itself to permit institutional change. The normative lifecycle would stumble upon the roadblocks created by the ruling regime, which prevents it from full development. Partial regime mimicry would signify an even lesser degree of democratization since the created institutional change will be considerably less durable and will not even partially serve their purpose but will exist as a mere mockery.

The way to overcome the problem of full or partial mimicry, i.e., to fill the form with the content, lies through a long-lasting and fundamental cultural change. Norm internalization will only happen under full-scale cultural transformations, which should transcend all the societal layers and sediment deep in the core of the individual identity of the nations. A good example of a successful internalization—and in quite a short period of time—is the transformation of Germany from supporting the Nazi regime into a democratic and egalitarian society shortly after World War II. For this process, two aspects are necessary. First, the external support in the form of knowledge transfers and economic assistance of the democratically developed nations to the newly democratizing societies will install and help sustain the institutional change through the norm emergence to the norm cascading. Second, the indomitable will of the nations and their governments, as the "norm entrepreneurs," is needed not only to accept the institutional changes and live through them without altering their political direction, but also to make the change an inherent part of their future identity. If both of these variables are present, the process of regime mimicry will move beyond democratic norm cascading to their internalization by creating and sustaining the identity imprints.

Ukraine, Georgia, and Belarus are at various stages of democratization and engage in diverse types of regime mimicries. The early years of their independence were quite turbulent, institutionally speaking. The three countries were plunged into the unknown and, therefore, by default an unsafe regional and international environment. No longer was the responsibility for decisionmaking and the behavior on the international arena being kept in Moscow: Ukraine, Georgia, and Belarus became individually in charge of their independent existence. The environment they appeared in at that time was highly unpredictable for them since they never fully existed as independent entities. In a habitat full of uncertainty and unpredictability, the three countries had chosen the institutional frameworks of democracy based on a number of reasons, which were different in each case.

Regime Mimicry in Ukraine.

In Ukraine, the process of democratic normative lifecycle was stalled at the stage of norm cascading. While local institutions have the designs and forms of democratic governance, they are not backed up by effectively conducted reforms, which will contribute to the normative spillovers in different areas. Some sectors are more advanced in their mimicry than others. The best example of this discrepancy, which is also within the separate components of the same sectors, is economic reforms. According to Marcin Święcicki:

> After 2 decades of transition, Ukraine is still far behind countries that joined the EU, including the three Baltic States, in economic reforms. . . . The most advanced areas in Ukraine's transition to a market economy by 2010 were small-scale privatization, price liberalization, and trade and the foreign exchange system. The least advanced were governance and enterprise restructuring, competition policy, and infrastructure.[225]

The same pessimistic tendency is noted in the case study, "Lessons from the Ukrainian Transition":

> [P]ositive developments in reform were not accompanied by a level of structural reform sufficient to guarantee a return to real economic growth . . . or to eliminate widespread distortions, non-payment and barter transactions, and rent seeking, particularly in the energy sector and in energy-intensive industries. Moreover, the government tolerated, and even encouraged, non-monetary transactions and even, to some extent, non-payments.[226]

The start of the democratic institutionalization process in Ukraine was similar to most of the post-Soviet republics: it, too, was expecting some benefits from joining the league of advanced European democracies. The external incentives model seemed to be working for Ukraine for quite some time. Out of the three models of isomorphism discussed previously, the first two — mimetic — was more applicable in the Ukrainian case. It has been receiving signals from the European community of having palpable advantages of behaving as democracies do, the most recent being the upcoming free trade agreement with the EU. Domestic actors also supported the democratic institutionalization to a point where more decisive steps should have been taken with regards to moving away from the external incentives toward the social learning and lesson-drawing model. There the process was interrupted by two factors: change of the government in Ukraine and the subsequent adjustments of the geopolitical orientation of the country after the failure of the Orange Revolution.

The general political course of integration with the European structures was somewhat reversed after the government change in 2010 with the addition of a clearly pro-Russian direction. The democratic world continues to assist Ukraine with institutional support, but the effectiveness of the reforms is lowered by a number of factors. First of all, it is the considerably large size of the country when compared with Georgia and Belarus that makes it difficult to effectively affect the institutional settings. Next is the regional divide, which diversified the popular responses to the proposed change. Finally, it is the internal ambiguity within the institutional actors as to how the country should develop further and the fluctuation of the domestic political environment.

This factor of geographic political preferences also affects the choice of the two logics. On the one hand, the government clearly sees the tangible economic and political benefits of democratic direction, including institutional socialization. On the other hand, however, the preferences are divided by the unique Ukrainian identity split between the West and the East, which prevents it from following both behavioral logics; it is impossible to credibly evaluate the pros and cons of either direction as well as to force the diverse parts of the country to follow a single course. The external incentives model that was working under the logic of consequentiality is further burdened by the fact of multiple rational preferences. The real question is whether Ukraine will eventually manage to mold a single political identity based on the mix of the two logics. This would also define the general political line: integration with the West/Europe or with the East/Russia.

The regime mimicry here is partial, but it is still a preferred way of interaction between the institutional actors, on the one hand, and the international community on the other. It is quite difficult to implement a change of political culture in such a large country as Ukraine. It would take much longer for the norm cascading and internalization due to the high diversity of the domestic political and cultural terrain. On the other hand, the relative rigidity of the Ukrainian political culture significantly contributes to the internal political stability of the country.

Regime Mimicry in Georgia.

In the case of Georgia, the mimicry is complex and omnipresent since it transcends all societal layers and is present in most societal functions. Externally available institutional designs were proposed to Georgia by international organizations (such as the EU, NATO, World Bank, etc.) in the form of various institutional incentives and reforms (educational, military, healthcare, to name a few) via financial support and knowledge transfers. While these reforms started during Shevardnadze's time, they accelerated with Saakashvili's ascent to power and his rigorous implementation of them.

From the point of view of the stimuli behind the regime mimicry, Georgia chose a combination of isomorphism—coercive, mimetic, and normative. It took the path towards democratization by combining the external incentives model (membership in international and regional organizations, grants, and credits) with the social learning (cultural change) and lesson-drawing (internal development) models. In doing so, Georgia was guided by the symbiosis of the two logics. The logic of consequentiality brought in the rational choice reasoning of expected rewards associated with acceptance of the institutional designs (such as further integration into the European structures including its possible membership in NATO) and punishments following possible defection from the accepted normative behavioral patterns. The logic of appropriateness, on its part, fostered real cultural change via a mentality transformation from that of a corrupt post-Soviet republic into an advanced democratic nation.

Anti-corruption activity, judiciary reform, revision of taxation—these are a few examples of institutional norm emergence. The process of norm cascading started with the gradual transformation of Georgian society where the spillovers went beyond their functional areas and started affecting an increasing number of institutions. For instance, corruption, a typical Soviet-type Georgian institution, was eradicated not only in law enforcement or judiciary but also in education, health, urban planning, etc. According to Alexander Kupatadze:

> [C]orruption has been substantially reduced in sectors where citizens interact with the state more frequently, including registering property, acquiring passports and licenses, and the police and the tax administration,[227]

in other words, everywhere where socialization between the electorate and the regime was the highest.

The process of full norm internalization, however, has not taken place yet. One reason is that the political culture requires a much longer period for cementing the change than the two election cycles after the Rose Revolution. The biggest change in the political culture of the Georgian elite was the nonacceptance of election fraud, which is widely spread in most post-Soviet societies. Jim Nichol called the 2012 parliamentary elections in Georgia "the first in the South Caucasus resulting in competitive and peaceful transfer of power,"[228] a totally different picture from all previous elections elsewhere in the Caucasus precipitated with various intricate forms of election fraud. For the norm internalization to have a long-lasting effect, the transformations should affect the deeper fibers of society to a point of no return to previously existing norms.

Another factor decelerating norm internalization is emergence of the backward trends with Ivanishvili's government, which engaged in political reversals, including the random amnesty of some 9,000 prisoners sentenced during Saakashvili's governance almost immediately after the elections[229] — politically motivated detentions and lawsuits against the former officials (such as former Minister of Interior Vano Merabishvili) and those associated with Saakashvili's governance. These developments impede a full normative lifecycle from completion and prevent the regime mimicry from turning into the real democratic institutionalization.

The norm diffusion became possible due to Georgia's political culture, which is actively systaltic and constantly prone to change, both domestically generated or externally imposed. It is fluid and highly susceptible to adoption or "mimicking," at various time junctions, the externally presented institutional arrangements of the governance regimes by the political elites. The pace of a normative "lifecycle" is quite high in Georgia. However, in order to bring the partial mimicry into full and transform it into complete norm internalization, two factors are necessary: unweathering external support and the iron will of the domestic institutional actors. Georgia does possess the first set of requirements for democratic norm internalization. The future of the domestic politics, more specifically, the October 2013 presidential elections and, especially, their aftermath, will show how committed those actors are to retain democratic designs.

An unexpected but serious problem with regime mimicry can come from the side of external agents — the institutions that are mimicked — which treat their mimicking counterparts the way a fully functioning institution should. They assume, in a way, that if the institutions are created or adopt democratic practices, they are democratic by definition. They put unbearable weight of democratic responsibility on the mimicking countries, which appear not to be ready for such a momentous burden. In doing so, they fail (or do not want) to assume that the recipient countries are simply mimicking them, and the change has only been a facade. The closing speech of NATO Secretary General Rasmussen following the meetings of NATO Defense Ministers on June 5, 2013, is notable with this regard. When asked about the recent politically motivated persecution of the political opponents in Georgia by a Georgian journalist, he replied:

> We are following these developments with great concern. . . . I made clear, and Ministers made clear, that we take it for granted that the Georgian authorities will fully respect the fundamental principles of rule of law and will guarantee due process.[230]

Such a conniving attitude, in a sense, assumes that mimicking countries have fully passed all the stages of democratic norm institutionalization and views them as properly functioning entities fully performing according to the standards of the copied institutions, which is not always the case.

Regime Mimicry in Belarus.

In Belarus, regime mimicry is in its embryonic form — quite far from even norm emergence. The type of isomorphism that stands closest to the Belarusian model is mimetic. Under the conditions of inherent uncertainty on the international arena, which were exacerbated by the relatively "young" independent existence of Belarus, its governance has chosen democratic design as a formative model to follow without proper institutional socialization. The continuous autocratic reign of Lukashenka is cutting down any aspirations for coercive isomorphism: the regime is intractable to either internally initiated or rational stimuli or pressure imposed from outside. The external incentive model stopped working a long time ago when the advanced democracies were dissuaded in their attempts to bring Belarus into the host of Europe, where it belongs, normatively and geographically speaking.

As early as in 1997, the EU froze its Partnership and Cooperation Agreement with Belarus in response to:

> the political situation in the country — most recently the violations of electoral standards in Belarus' presidential elections (2010) and the ensuing crackdown on civil society, political opposition, and independent media.[231]

This is because the autocratic governance coercively impedes the external incentives from being properly diffused among institutional actors who had never had a chance to enact the social learning, let alone the lesson-drawing models. None of the two logics were at work here: the benefits for acting democratically are not clearly visible or available for the domestic actors to start behaving appropriately. Belarusian autocracy manages to block successfully both the external support in the form of transfers of democratization designs and the institutional actors from expressing their free will for change.

There are, of course, some signs of institutional designs of the democratic governance in Belarus, such as dispersed civil society and quite nominal human rights protection mechanisms. However, neither of them is fully efficient. Even worse so, they are sporadic, nonsystemic, and subject to strict internal oversight. Belarus has accepted democratic institutions mostly by their form, while utterly disregarding their contexts. For example, according to its constitutions, Belarus is "a unitary, democratic, social state based on the rule of law" where "[t]he individual, his rights, freedoms and guarantees to secure them are the supreme value and goal of the society and the State" and its people are "the sole source of state power and the bearer of sovereignty in the Republic of Belarus."[232] In reality, however, Lukashenka is the alpha and omega of domestic authority in the country, allowing for no contextual or substantial transfer of the institutional meaning.

At the same time, Belarus, too, imitates the externally proposed institutional frameworks, but there is an important difference between the two types of mimicry. In Georgia and to a certain degree in Ukraine, this process is deliberate and rational. These countries experience the influence of external constraints and opportunities by accepting certain institutional frameworks. Here the difference is that the autocratic governance blurs Belarus' vision of tangible benefits from full democratic institutionalization. The authoritarian political culture shows a significantly higher degree of rigidity than in Georgia and Ukraine. It has no strictly defined regional identity but fully depends on the will of Lukashenka, who tries to balance at the brink of different extremes for the personal benefits and those of his close cycle.

With all the difficulty of dealing with Europe and the recent worsening of the relations with Russia over the possession of and control over "Belaruskali." One of the Belarusian industrial giants producing significant amounts of world's potassium.[233] Belarus is turning for political and economic help elsewhere. The recent economic rapprochement with China (with the amount of U.S.$5.5 billion and another U.S.$30 billion in the future) marked another round in the political games of Lukashenka with the rest of the world. By calling China "the global empire," "the leading power of the world," and "the world's center,"[234] Lukashenka is sending clear political messages both to the West and Russia of keeping his options open and actively looking for a patron. This step signifies the political immaturity of Lukashenka's regime, which negatively affects the process of international mimicry: the level of international involvement in Belarus in the form of institutional or fiscal support is extremely small and equally nonsystemic. Overall, the resistance to political evolution reflects the increased institutional path-dependency in Belarus in withstanding the environmental changes and preventing conscious institutional socialization. The pace of normative "life-cycles" there is lethargic and subject to the limitations of the Belarusian respective political culture, which makes its societies immune to multiple short-term regime changes.

"INPUTS" VERSUS "OUTPUTS"

In most of the advanced democracies, there is a dual connection between democratic governance and political stability. Democratic institutions with their norms, rules, and practices put in place centuries ago as a result of human evolution create the necessary conditions for both internal and external political stability. Democratic governance builds up the environment for equal political participation and fair treatment for all the citizens. A social contract existing in the democracies is based on the notion of positive trust existing between the government and its citizens. The citizens trust the government in its observance of the terms of the social contract by offering physical and property protection, as well as observing the human rights and fundamental principles. This is done by creating and respecting the checks-and-balances in the government, as well as keeping the government accountable via holding regular free and fair elections. The government, for its part, trusts the citizens in their fulfillment of the terms of the social contract by respecting its decisions and not revolting against them.

Advanced democratic governance regimes also contribute to the external stability of their countries by decreasing the possibility and effectiveness of foreign interference in their domestic affairs. The positive trust presents itself by the increased public cohesion in face of the threat coming from outside as well as preventing their governments from starting arbitrary wars. Under the constraints established by democratic designs, the ruling government would have to go through lengthy procedures of authorizing use of force abroad. In addition, democratic governments must comply with the global and regional governance regimes, having established the world order that (at least nominally) respects the principles of state sovereignty, nonintervention into the domestic affairs of other states, and the supremacy of the human rights protection system.

The situation is radically different in autocracies. There, the internal political stability is based on the negative trust instilled by the fear of the citizens that they would definitely be worse off if they show disagreement with the ruling regimes. The governments consider any public activity of its citizens as suspicious by definition, and the former fear that any actions will necessarily have punitive backlashes on the part of their governments. Thus, the stability of autocracies is measured by their ability to coerce effectively their own citizens into compliance with the existing institutional arrangements. This usually makes political culture apathetic and discourages political experiments. Internal durability of the autocratic regimes also depends on individual leadership, where the autocrats via their close cycles of family and affiliates represent the sole source of legitimacy and stability for the countries and their citizens. The change of autocratic leadership usually leads to at least short-term political disturbance, depending on the specific interplay of domestic power groups.

From the point of view of external political stability, the autocratic governance is much less stable than its democratic counterpart. Autocratic leaders tend to show more contrariness in defining their foreign policy priorities by the virtue of having much fewer constraints due to the absence or ineffective checks-and-balances systems. The reason is that the constituencies have far fewer possibilities to participate in the domestic and foreign lives of their countries under the pressure of their autocratic governance and to block the undesired actions of their governments.

The process of governance is a two-way reciprocal dialogue between the ruling regime and institutional actors. In order to be effective, democratic governance should provide for the protection of the rights of their citizens and also ensure their free and uninterrupted participation in the political life of their country. The second part of the effective governance is contained in the efforts the citizenry makes to contribute to this process. Bo Rothstein and Jan Teorell call these two components of democracy as "inputs" and "outputs." According to them:

> A state regulates relations to its citizens on two dimensions. One is the 'input' side, which relates to access to public authority. The other is the 'output' side and refers to the way in which that authority is exercised.[235]

On the more contextual level, the outputs and inputs are closely connected with the notion of the social contract where outputs are about the benefits the citizens will get from the government in case of their compliance as well as the punishments they would receive in case of defection from their governments' rule, and inputs are enshrined in the process of participation of the citizenry in governance processes.

Effective interplay between outputs and inputs has direct consequences for the overall sustainability of the governance regimes discussed by Lipset. In his equation, outputs are tantamount to regime effectiveness, and inputs are related to the notion of governments' legitimacy. Democracies exercise political equality on the combined inputs and outputs sides of their social contracts. Equal democratic participation of the citizens in the form of the inputs provides for the basis of norms, rules, and practices of democratic institutionalization. Impartial outputs cement the equality between the citizens as exercised by the democratically elected authorities. The inputs, in a sense, are the bases of the fulfillment of the "social contracts" since they represent the media of participation of the institutional actors in the lives of their countries.

In autocracies, the linkages between inputs and outputs are distorted by authoritarian resilience. On the one hand, autocracies do not allow for outputs to be available to all layers of society. Unlike democratic equality, autocracies provide higher outputs for close cycles of governance and discriminate against all the rest and much lower outputs for the rest of the population. Correspondingly, the effectiveness and legitimacy of authoritarian regimes are based on inputs from those cycles alone, which mostly have to do with the individual loyalty to the regimes and their leaders. Under autocratic governance, institutional actors do not produce or are restricted from full provision of the inputs, whereas outputs are skewed in favor of the ruling elites.

Autocracies may remain stable for some time by providing lone outputs, which will satisfy the main human requirements for the institutional actors, as stated by Abraham Maslow.[236] At the same time, they would have to compensate for the inputs by mimicking the democratic institutional forms without creating viable conditions for full and equal participation of the actors in the political processes. In situations with high outputs but low inputs, there is a risk of the governance to turn into some form of authoritarian regime. Not fearing popular discontent, governments may provide for the basic or even higher needs of their societies, while keeping their political participation to a minimum. On the contrary, low outputs combined with high inputs, which is a perfect precondition for state failure, would increase the proclivity of popular uprisings. Not satisfied with the current economic conditions, the public may consolidate against their governments.

The future of the democratization/political stability/economic development nexus in Ukraine, Georgia, and Belarus can be explored by relating it to the inputs versus outputs discourse on democratization from the point of view of the characteristics of their regime mimicries. Ideally, the levels of outputs should be equal to those of inputs. The reason why the regime mimicry is more advanced in Georgia, partial in Ukraine, and rudimentary in Belarus is because democracy is only possible where there are both inputs and outputs; without either of these components, it will only be partial and unviable.

Ukraine.

The duality of its political culture had affected negatively the prospects for internal and external political stability. Internally, the current government is in charge of the political processes and due to the overwhelming popular apathy, faces a low threat from the increased political activity of the opposition. The Orange Revolution–type euphoria has long ago sunk into oblivion. Only serious internal economic and/or political shocks can pose any significant threats to the ruling regime. The partial regime mimicry allows the current government to provide for the basic needs of its population in the form of outputs: jobs available to most of the population with the unemployment level as low as 1.6 percent of the total population;[237] and relatively decent healthcare, education, and communal services. These outputs are offered to the wider societal layers, although to a much more limited scale than in Belarus. There is still inflation that has to be dealt with, making it difficult for the government to sustain decent economic levels with current economic policies. Further reforms are necessary with regard to economic revival. This is very difficult to undertake without substantial external support. Ukraine has to make a serious decision quite soon about its foreign policy direction.

The input side of democratic institutionalization is also present but is limited due to the political apathy of the institutional actors, which prevents them from inflicting large-scale internal political change. Current actions of the political opposition are sporadic and nonsystemic, which is further aggravated by the internal political rifts between the key opposition parties. Vitali Kilichko's recent announcement to run for president may act as a significant wake-up call for the Ukraine's anemic political life from the point of view of uniting the opposition and increasing the inputs side of democratization. This move will most definitely face the highly tenaciousness current governance. Yet, the chronic apathy would prevent another revolutionary scenario from happening.

From the point of view of external political stability, popular political lethargy aggravates the limbo of the Ukrainian political establishment to choose a foreign policy course. As reflected in a Congressional Research Service memo, the:

> conflict between Ukraine's political forces has led its foreign policy to appear incoherent, as the contend-

ing forces pulled it in pro-Western or pro-Russia directions. . . . Ukrainian leaders gave lip service to joining NATO and the European Union, but did little to meet the standards set by these organizations. Ukrainian leaders also promised closer ties with Russia in exchange for Russian energy at subsidized prices, but balked at implementing agreements with Russia that would seriously compromise Ukraine's sovereignty. . . .[238]

In practical terms, it translates into Yanukovych's dropping NATO's membership action plan (MAP) aspirations of Yushchenko without any significantly important steps towards economic, political, and cultural integration with Russia or with the EU.

Georgia.

Internal political stability in Georgia may be shaken by possible future abrupt and largely unexpected governmental changes and the resulting "tilting" of the main political axis towards rapprochement with Russia. Many of the recent moves made by Ivanishvili's new government, including statements blaming Saakashvili for starting the war with Russia,[239] the declared participation in the 2014 Olympic Games, resumption of wine exports to Russia, and the release of prisoners, while not openly anti-Western, show the "gaps" in the volatile domestic political culture.

The signs of "thawing" of relations with Russia are directed mostly at gaining popular support at home by reviving the economic and cultural nostalgia of older generations of Georgians with Russia. The new government is making some steps to reestablish the political, economic, and cultural relations with Russia,[240] which is not well-received by a considerable part of the Georgian population. Quite recently, Ivan-ishvili promised to follow another geopolitical course: towards integration with NATO, while blaming Georgian society in a "low level of political culture."[241] This move seems quite out of touch with the real geopolitical situation. Ever since Putin's second presidential term, anti-NATO rhetoric firmly entered the internal political discourse in Russia. NATO retains the highest threat level for Russian statehood, as viewed both by its military and politicians. Russia would, thus, do everything in its power not to border NATO with Georgia being its member.

The deployment of NATO radar installations in Eastern Europe is one of the highest irritants for Russia. According to Commander of the Moscow Antimissile Defense Major General Vladimir Lyaporov, "the only guarantee for . . . [Russia] is the complete halt by the U.S. of deploying its missile defense systems in Europe."[242] One of the most outspoken critics of NATO, Dmitri Rogozin, former Russian representative to the Alliance, echoed the military's view in saying:

> We will, of course, build the system that would overcome and suppress any anti-missile defense. If anyone thinks that we can be surrounded by a missile fence, let them recall: under Peter [the Great] we 'cut through the window' to Europe, and now we will crush the whole wall, if someone tries to isolate us or tries to bring us to our knees.[243]

From this perspective, not only the two currently proposed directions (Russia versus NATO) cannot be pursued simultaneously, but they are quite oxymoronic by definition.

In addition, some of the most important pre-election promises of the Georgian Dream — economic revival and improvement of the social climate in the country—have not yet been put into life. According to the recent NDI public opinion poll, most of the respondents do not see significant changes in the situation in Georgia after Ivanishvili's election. The promised increase of the output side of governance, including low prices for gasoline, decreased unemployment (from the registered towering 15 percent in 2012),[244] consumer products, and communal services, has been thwarted, which explains the growing disillusionment of Georgian society with the performance of their current government. With the hectic and non-systemic movements in domestic politics, the number of those becoming dissuaded with current government is slowly growing. All these make the October 2013 presidential elections another test for the domestic political stability via the democratic inputs. The incongruence between the high inputs and low outputs may endanger an already volatile domestic political environment, especially in light of the elections.

The reality is: Saakashvili's two presidential terms are over; his nominee, Vano Merabishvili, ex-Prime Minister and ex-Minister of Interior, is detained by the new government with charges of corruption and abuse of power. This, however, does not mean that Saakashvili's party is beheaded. David Bakradze, a young pro-Western politician and the former Chair of Parliament, has been nominated as a presidential candidate from the United National Movement. The candidate of the Georgian Dream, Giorgi Margvelashvili, is relatively well known to the Georgian political establishments as a person involved in the democratic processes while working at the NDI and the Georgian Institute of Public Affairs (GIPA'96), the first American-type higher educational institution in Georgia.[245]

Had the presidential elections been held immediately after the successful parliamentary début of the Georgian Dream, their results might have depended largely on public euphoria. Now the situation has somewhat changed: the inability of the new government to bring quick and visible economic outputs for their population has shaken the political scale towards increased political uncertainty and, as a result, the high propensity for the intensification of negative inputs in different forms of popular protests.

External threats to political stability, on the other hand, ceased after the war with Russia in 2008. With the acknowledgement of the independence of Abkhazia and South Ossetia by Russia, their de facto territorial loss for Georgia turned into the de jure separation of these territories. This also means a paradoxically stabilizing development from the point of view of the absence of the external threat. For more than 2 decades, Georgia has been living under constant fear of a Russian invasion, which was reaffirmed by numerous sporadic bombings of its northern districts bordering Chechnya. This factor significantly affected internal political processes and economic development. Now that the frozen conflicts in the secessionist regions have been somewhat resolved, the threat of resumption of hostilities is quite low. This stance is corroborated by a recent survey by NDI, in which only 26 percent of respondents consider Russia a threat, while another 42 percent believe that this threat is exaggerated, and 23 percent more thinks that Russia is no longer a threat to Georgia.[246]

Belarus.

The outputs-inputs imbalance of democratic governance is important in analyzing the longevity of the current governance regime in Belarus. By covering mostly the outputs satisfying limited and elementary demands of its population, Lukashenka's authoritarian social contract managed to survive throughout the first decades of post-Soviet existence. These outputs in the form of relatively high economic benefits, very low unemployment (0.6 percent of the total population),[247] decent education, healthcare, communal services, etc., are on an acceptable level for the public, which increases the legitimacy of the authoritarian regime among the majority of institutional actors. One such visible output mentioned by the *Global Peace Index 2013* of the Institute of Economics and Peace is the low level of criminality, which satisfies the basic safety/security strata of the Maslow pyramid. The inputs side of the state-citizenry interaction is restricted to sporadic expressions of popular unrest, which are quickly put down by the punitive state apparatus. The regime is highly effective in precluding any form and content of the public participation not agreed upon with Lukashenka's close circles.

Widely acceptable outputs and almost absolute absence of political inputs on the part of the institutional actors created a special type of social contract in Belarus based on the policy of intimidation and popular content. This, in turn, breeds apathy and indifference to the political situation inside the country. In Silitski's words, Belarus "secures civil peace and political stability, which justifies limitations on some civil freedoms."[248] The social contract in Belarus is thus based on fear and en masse intimidations, coupled with high autocratic resilience, which jointly represent the very mechanisms preventing the democratic norms from full emergence, let alone their cascading and socialization. The regime mimicry is embryonic in Belarus, which is evident in the forms and names of governance tools (president, parliament, the system of courts, constitution, etc.) that do not fully fulfill their designated purpose.

From the point of view of internal and external political stability, Belarus is also the most politically consolidated and homogenous if compared with Georgia and Ukraine. It is not divided either by ethnic, ideological, or geographic lines: the country is unvaried concerning its ethnic composition and rock solid with its geopolitical preferences. Years of balancing between Europe and Russia created a very pragmatic foreign policy directed to serve the sole task of prolongation of the durability of Lukashenka's regime. Unlike Ukraine, there is no internal right between the geographic political orientation of the country. Unlike Georgia, there are not threats to the territorial integrity of Belarus internally or from outside. This fact also contributes to the political stability of Belarus by limiting the external threats to Lukashenka's regime.

POLICY IMPLICATIONS FOR THE UNITED STATES

Ultimately, it is the political cultures of Ukraine, Georgia, and Belarus that define the durability of their political regimes and variations in their democratic institutionalization. The U.S. policy towards these countries should be based on the acknowledgment of the phenomenon of diverse political cultures as having decisive influence over the political processes in these countries. Out of the three countries, Georgia is the closest ally of the United States, politically and militarily speaking. It has been a recipient of significant economic and military aid from the United States, including the training and equipment of its elite military units. Ukraine, too, has been cooperating militarily with the United States, but mostly via the international channels of NATO. Together, Georgia and Ukraine have been active participants of joint international military peacekeeping efforts, such as the U.S.-led coalitions in Afghanistan and Iraq. Belarus, on the other hand, follows the general "outlier" trajectory by being the least cooperating state with the U.S. military structures. Its involvement with the "former adversaries" is limited to its participation in the NATO PfP exercise.

Ukraine.

The situation in Ukraine deserves close attention from the United States. Ukraine as a stable country, both politically and economically, is in direct U.S. interests, with its considerable stakes in general European political stability and global peace. Ukraine is an important hub on the way between the East and West in terms of cultural, economic, and political interactions. According to Mark Kramer, having Ukraine as a democracy would be:

> a firm barrier against any attempt to restore the Soviet Union. . . . On the other hand, the United States has sought to diminish and forestall tensions between Ukraine and Russia and to ensure that the two large, neighboring states live peacefully together.[249]

Traditionally, the United States has been keenly interested in keeping the stability in Ukraine from several perspectives: ensuring the regional nuclear nonproliferation, safeguarding human rights and civil society development, and supporting its economic independence.

Early U.S. concerns in Ukraine were framed by post–Cold War nuclear nonproliferation initiatives. Ukraine was one of the few Soviet republics left with a nuclear arsenal after its dissolution. As Dubovyk states:

> If there was one absolute priority for the United States during the collapse of the Soviet Union, it was to stabilize the situation of the former Soviet Union's nuclear weapons.[250]

Soon after Ukraine's independence, the U.S. administration focused on improving cooperation in such fields as nuclear nonproliferation and safe nuclear energy. So far, the United States contributed the cumulative sum of more than U.S.$360 million to decontamination of the Chornobyl nuclear disaster.[251] Within the framework of the 1993 "Nunn-Lugar" Cooperative Threat Reduction Program, the United States:

> provide[s] equipment, services and technical advice to assist Ukraine in preventing proliferation and in securing and dismantling weapons of mass destruction, related materials, and production facilities inherited from the former Soviet Union.[252]

More recently, while congratulating Yanukovych with his presidency, President Barack Obama reiterated the 2008 United States-Ukraine Charter on Strategic Partnership, while noting the main themes of U.S. policy toward Ukraine:

> [e]xpanding democracy and prosperity, protecting security and territorial integrity, strengthening the rule of law, promoting non-proliferation, and supporting reform in Ukraine's economic and energy sectors.[253]

The United States is particularly vigilant and "deeply disappointed" with the human rights situation in Ukraine, in particularly, the "politically motivated prosecution" of the prominent opposition figures, such as Tymoshenko.[254] U.S. Congress H. Res. 730 (2012) calls for tougher reaction on the part of the U.S. Government, including denial to issue visas to Ukrainian officials:

> involved in serious human rights abuses, anti-democratic actions, or corruption that undermines or injures democratic institutions in Ukraine, including officials responsible for and participating in the selective prosecution and persecution of political opponents.[255]

The United States is also concerned with the general condition of civil society, including its inputs in the democratic process, among others, via their election participation. In the Department of State statement after the October 2012 elections, the U.S. Government called the election a "step backward" from the previous progress and regretfully noted "the use of government resources to favor ruling party candidates, interference with media access, and harassment of opposition candidates."[256]

Economic well-being of Ukraine, including its energy independence from Russia, is also on the U.S. agenda. Ukraine is a member of the Partnership and

Cooperation Agreement (PCA) with the EU and the Ukraine-EU Action Plan within the European Neighborhood policy. It is the major area connecting Russian gas with European markets, and its internal and external political stability depends largely on the energy security of Europe. According to Gunther Oettinger, the EU Commissioner for Energy, Ukraine has the potential to become "the Eastern European gas hub" with its "significant gas resources, both conventional and unconventional, together with the vast networks of gas pipelines already in place and important gas storage capacities."[257] Economically, too, a strong Ukraine is a guarantee for the retention of democratic values. The current trade blackmail by Russia as a response to the mere fact that "the most pro-Russian of all possible Ukrainian leaderships no longer wants to be friends with Moscow by the Russian rules and wants to sneak away to Europe"[258] shows the possible worsening of the domestic economic climate. This may add up to the economic hardships of the population and, as a result, bring it closer to the brink of political protests. Any dependence of Ukraine on Russia concerning the gas supplies as well as economic development will negatively affect the domestic economic settings in Europe and, ultimately, its energy security.

The U.S. Government should continue its efforts to support civil society, economic development, and the ongoing rule of law initiatives, such as the democratization grants, various sector-specific economic assistance programs, and the media development fund grants. All these programs will further contribute to the strengthening of the input sides of democratic institutionalization. Existence of relative internal and external political stability allows for long-term programs currently being supported. The United States should also closely work with the Ukrainian government in the matter of deepening the integration of the country in the international structures, such as the EU and NATO.

The Ukrainian-U.S. military relations, according to Leonid Polyakov, are directed at:

> help[ing] in building a stable, prosperous democracy that can become a viable economic and security partner to the West . . . within the bilateral military-to-military contacts programs, within NATO partnership events, and through the practical accomplishment of peacekeeping and humanitarian missions.[259]

Ukraine is involved in military cooperation with the American, in particular, and Western, in general, military structures primarily through the channels of international organizations (mostly NATO).

Ukraine is an active participant in international military exercises and international peacekeeping efforts. Ukrainian contribution to the "Coalition of the Willing" in Iraq included the cumulative 7,000 soldiers, with the peak deployment of 1,630.[260] Its membership in the ISAF in Afghanistan is limited to 22 soldiers. Overall, according to the Ministry of Defense of Ukraine, the country is involved in 11 peacekeeping missions and other international operations with the current total of 476 servicemen.[261] Ukraine also is quite active in joint military exercises with regional and international partners, such as "Peace Shield," "Rapid Trident," "Sea Breeze" (with NATO and Partners for Peace countries), "Cossack Steppe" (Ukraine-United Kingdom [UK]-Poland), "Maple Arch" (Ukraine-Canada-Poland-Lithuania), "Blackseafor," "Light Avalon" (Ukraine-Hungary-Romania-Slovak), "Rescuer/Medcuer," and "Jackal Stone 2011,"[262] to name a few.

Contributing involvement of Ukraine in international peacekeeping efforts is based on its cooperation framework with NATO, regulated by the NATO-Ukraine Special Partnership Charter (1997), the engine of which is the NATO-Ukraine Commission. The Commission is tasked with fostering military cooperation and consultations between the Alliance countries and Ukraine within international military peacekeeping engagement. Its main purpose is to promote technical cooperation with Ukraine in the field of armaments; foster civil emergency planning; and encourage public information sharing and scientific cooperation. Subsequently, the Commission established sector-specific instruments as the Joint Working Group on Defense Reform (JWGDR) responsible for military-to-military cooperation (1998), NATO-Ukraine Working Group on Civil and Democratic Control of the Intelligence Sector and Partnership Network for Civil Society Expertise Development (2006).

Ukraine was the first among the former Soviet republics to join the PfP endeavor in 1994. In the aftermath of the Orange Revolution, Ukraine started expressing increasing desire for close integration with the Alliance, which manifested in the Intensified Dialogue with NATO (2005) and the general agreement of the Alliance members expressed at the NATO Bucharest Summit (2008) to accept Ukraine as its member in the future. The direction towards NATO membership was abandoned with the change of the government in 2010: according to Steven Woehrel, "Yanukovych has made clear that his country is not seeking NATO membership, but is continuing to cooperate with NATO, including the holding of joint military exercises"[263] — two steps back and one step forward.

The military side of the bilateral U.S. cooperation with Ukraine, according to Polyakov, is based on the following set of its core interests:

> U.S. willingness to support the preservation of Ukraine's independence as a key to regional security and Ukrainian willingness to cooperate with the United States in fighting terrorism and preserving international peace.[264]

These interests are further formulated in a number of bilateral documents defining their cooperation frameworks, among which the most important were concluded on international assistance programs and projects in military sphere (1999); on exchange of research and development information in the sphere of military technical cooperation (2000); and on transfer of military equipment and rendering of services (2004).

The framework cooperation principles are presented by the U.S.-Ukraine Charter on Strategic Partnership. Section II focuses on bilateral military cooperation aimed, first and foremost, at bringing Ukraine closer to NATO through enacting a:

> structured plan to increase interoperability and coordination of capabilities between NATO and Ukraine, including via enhanced training and equipment for Ukrainian armed forces.[265]

The U.S. European Command (EUCOM), through the Office of Defense Cooperation, provides "military equipment and training to support the modernization of Ukraine's military."[266] These activities include, but are not limited to, Joint Contact Team Program-Ukraine (JCTP) (deployment of the U.S. troops to share their experience with their Ukrainian colleagues); International Military Education and Training (IMET) (training of the Ukrainian military and affiliated civilian personnel in the U.S. to foster closer partnership with NATO), and Foreign Military Sales and Financing (economic assistance to defense reforms).

The prospects of the military cooperation between the United States and Ukraine will be, without a doubt, influenced by the third party, Russia. Seeing itself as "one of the most influential and competitive centers of the world" and having conceptually "negative opinion on the NATO enlargement and approach of NATO military infrastructure to the Russian borders,"[267] Russia is vitally interested in diminishing military cooperation of the former Soviet republics—especially bordering it—with NATO, in general, and the United States, in particular. Ukraine is the last outpost of Russia in the Western direction, the last "buffer" between NATO and Russia, and is, therefore, treated by the latter with particular attention. Recently, for example, Russia accused Ukraine of supplying arms to Georgia prior to war in 2008.[268] The deal, which was viewed by the Russian political and military establishment as having been fostered by the United States and which, therefore, was received with extreme discontent. Although some renowned experts on Soviet Union, including Brzezinski, consider that "[t]oday's Russia is in no position to assert a violent restoration of its old empire. It is too weak, too backward and too poor,"[269] it would still try to do its best to influence foreign policy courses of those former Soviet republics who are weaker, poorer, and more backward that itself.

If Russia manages successfully to coerce Ukraine to move away from its association with the EU and closer to its Customs Union, this would mark a turning point in the future political orientation of Ukraine, as the largest Eastern European country. This would inevitably affect its military cooperation with the Alliance and its member-states, including the United States. Therefore, the United States should intensify its military cooperation and partnership with Ukraine to keep it true to its choice of democratization and from reverting the course towards the military reforms and overall military progress.

Georgia.

The future of the political stability in Georgia depends on the sustainability of the initial institutional transformations: the will of the domestic polity and the durability of the political culture to internal and external shocks. Currently, in Jack Goldstone's terms, in Georgia the:

> popularly elected government . . . is seen to be pursuing just policies [that] can survive for some years even if it has difficulty delivering on its programs, while it struggles to strengthen its capacities to govern.[270]

The regime mimicry has not yet gone through the final stage of the normative process and is now threatened by the fluid political identity that may adversely affect the previously made democratic progress. Reversal of the political courses in Georgia is fraught with irreversible consequences.

The United States is vitally interested in keeping Georgia politically stable. During Saakashvili's governance, to a certain degree, the United States acted as a role model for Georgia and the major financial and moral supporter for its institutional reforms. It has been a consistent lobby of the Georgian political course towards democratization for the past 2 decades. It has been supporting its democratization efforts by providing economic, educational, political, and cultural assistance. Some programs, such as the USAID-funded "Georgia Community Mobilization Initiative" in 2000-05, were multi-million dollar efforts to transform Georgian society by increasing its inputs in its daily lives and keeping its elected leaders accountable for their actions. Largely to its credit, Georgia was able to keep the beacon of democracy turned on through its October 2012 parliamentary elections.

Continuous U.S. support via active dialogue with all domestic political forces is required to sustain the democratic institutionalization process in Georgia. The United States should further encourage democratization efforts of Georgia by holding constant dialogue with all the participants of the political process to avoid possible short- and long-term destabilization. The United States should continue fostering the reform processes, primarily in the field of institutional and economic development and human rights protection. The current programs, such as the ongoing democratization grants and other sector-specific programs (Democracy Commission grants, democracy outreach, media partnership, economic developmental aid via USAID; the activities of the Millennium Challenge Corporation directed to the poverty reduction and economic growth; education exchange programs; mass media support programs, etc.) should be reinforced. Tackling different areas of the democratic development process will strengthen regime mimicry and move it towards norm internalization. In addition, this would contribute significantly to the increased participation of the institutional actors in the "input" part of the democratization design. The U.S. involvement will also positively influence internal political stability of Georgia by extending consultations and advice on democracy and economic development. Otherwise, the norm internalization will be stalled, and the mimicry process will revert to partial with unpredictable consequences. Under the worst-case scenario, the resulting situation may lead to a reversal of democratic gains.

Another priority direction for the U.S. interests in Georgia is its continuous integration within the Western political structures, including NATO. The democratization part of the NATO basket will ensure the steady implementation of reforms and preservation of the overall political orientation of the country. The April 2008 Bucharest Summit for the first time named Georgia (together with Ukraine) as an aspirant country and noted that it "will become a member of NATO," although it did not specify when exactly this would happen. The activities of the NATO-Georgia Commission (NGC) include political consultations and cooperation on assisting Georgia in its Euro-Atlantic integration processes. Georgia is a participant in the NATO Planning and Review Process (PARP) to further assist its democratic transition and has the Annual National Program (ANP) to provide frameworks for Georgia-NATO cooperation.

The U.S. actions in the matter of further integration of Georgia in NATO should continue with the cautious understanding of the sensitive relations of Georgia with Russia. The possible development closer to Russia would endanger this carefully created and nurtured cooperation with the North Alliance. The recent statement of Ivanishvili on his intent to obtain a NATO MAP for Georgia in 2014,[271] which many view as another stepping-stone on the path to the NATO membership, seems to reinforce the general foreign policy course of the country towards further democratization. However, in light of the moves of Georgia toward the other Russian direction, this statement seems less credible. Advocates for NATO membership for Georgia should not forget the outspokenly negative stance of Russian leadership on this issue. Russia has been a consistent antagonist to NATO, in general, and to its enlargement, in particular. These feelings exacerbated after Putin came to power in 2000. Prime Minister Dmitri Medvedev recently stated that possible membership in NATO "will not bring anything to Georgia as a sovereign and well-developing state but will create a long-term and constant source of tension between our countries."[272] Nevertheless, the United States should continue to support the aspirations of Georgia to join the progressive community of states under the aegis of NATO.

Georgia has been an active participant of the international military peacekeeping efforts. The Georgian contingent in the "Coalition of the Willing" in Iraq included the cumulative 10,000 soldiers with the peak deployment of 1,850.[273] With its 1,561 troops, Georgia is the largest per capita contributor to the ISAF in Afghanistan and has suffered the highest casualties among the Euro-Atlantic Partnership Council (EAPC) nations.[274] In addition, Georgia is deeply integrated into the international military organizations: it is participating in joint PfP endeavor within the frameworks of NATO and is involved in other multilateral military exercises in the region.

All this became possible as a result of the military cooperation with the United States, which started over a decade ago with the inception of the "Georgia

Train and Equip Program" (GTEP) in 2002-04. With the total cost of U.S.$64 million and the participation of 150 U.S. military experts,[275] the GTEP was placed to address the growing need of Georgia in securing its borders from the repeated Russian provocations, such as the numerous bombings of the Pankisi Gorge, a mountainous part of Georgia bordering Chechnya. The task of the GTEP was to train the Georgian soldiers in such areas as border security, anti-terrorism, and crisis response, as well as to foster the reform in the Georgian military sector. In addition to the training program, GTEP provided the country's military units with the most up-to-date military equipment, including "uniform items, small arms and ammunition, communications gear, training gear, medical gear, fuel, and construction materiel."[276] Altogether, 2,000 Georgian soldiers from four light infantry battalions and a mechanized company team were trained within the frameworks of the GTEP mission.

After the GTEP, another significant military assistance program is the Georgian Sustainment and Stability Operations Program (GSSOP) with an additional $159 million from 2005–08 to train three brigades of 2,000 soldiers and to provide the necessary military equipment, such as anti-improvised explosive devices (IEDs) and radios.[277] Also, the U.S. military assisted in reorganization and rehabilitation of the naval capabilities of the Georgian defense. The Georgia Border Security and Law Enforcement (GBLSE) and Export Control and Related Border Security (EXBS) programs (with U.S.$850,000 combined) provided assistance in repairing the Georgian fleet and maritime radar stations.[278] Finally, Georgia is included in the International Military Education and Training (IMET) Program, which provides training and education to the military students. Overall, from 2006-11, U.S. \$846,000 was spent on increasing the skills and knowledge of the Georgian military.[279]

Not surprisingly, such military cooperation between the United States and Georgia caused a harsh negative reaction in the Russian political establishment.[280] Tony Karon described the Russian reaction on the GTEP as "hopping mad."[281] The Russian fears were that Georgia would use the U.S.-trained military in operations in its breakaway regions of Abkhazia and South Ossetia. Also, as a part of the common anti-NATO paranoia in the Russian defense and policy circles, the GTEP program was considered as another step to a closer alignment of Georgia with the NATO. The Russian factor has to be taken very seriously into account in case of any future military assistance programs in Georgia. As the Russian government traditionally is highly suspicious of any American involvement in the region, which it considers its "own lot" and is not going to leave,[282] it is highly imperative that:

> the United States must move forward in a highly transparent manner, in coordination with our European and NATO allies, in order to dispel misinformation and to lessen any risk of miscalculation."[283]

With this negative Russian stance to the deepening partnership with the United States, in particular, and NATO, in general, the U.S. military should intensify its cooperation with Georgia. To put it bluntly, Georgia has run out of the territories that Russia can lay its claims on. There are no other parts of Georgia, except for Abkhazia and South Ossetia, which have been tightly integrated with Russia legally (through common Russian citizenship) and morally (through their external homelands), which can entice future Russian military involvements. This fact, together with the new seemingly more favorable Georgian government creates the conditions conducive to political stability in the mid- and possibly long-term. At the same time, the United States should reiterate its support to the territorial integrity in Georgia by mediating the non-aggression pact between Georgia and Russia on the international arena and during bilateral negotiations with both parties concerned.

The U.S. military should continue cooperation with Georgia within the frameworks of the U.S.-Georgia Charter on Strategic Partnership, which stresses the U.S. support to "the efforts of Georgia to provide for its legitimate security and defense needs, including development of appropriate and NATO-interoperable military forces."[284] Whereas the pre-2008 war NATO was hesitant to conduct real talks on the Georgian accession, the post-war NATO, with the U.S. impetus, should reinstate the return to the integration processes for Georgia. While NATO will remain as an ongoing irritant for the general Russian polity, it is highly unlikely that Russia will find another intervention pretext in Georgia in case of the further NATO enlargement efforts. This will also give a boost to the external democratic institutionalization efforts in Georgia and keep it true to the democratization reforms. At the same time, the United States and NATO should make it very clear to the Georgian leadership that they would not be willing to support the military actions of Georgia directed towards the return of the lost land: this would mean direct confrontation with Russia should be avoided.

Belarus.

Belarus has been also within the focus of the international community, but not because of its threat to regional stability or due to the high level of internal violence. Belarus is the most politically stable, internally and externally speaking, and economically developed (per capita) out of the three countries in the present analysis. Internally, Belarus represents Goldstone's case of the duality between effectiveness and legitimacy:

> States that have high levels of either effectiveness or legitimacy, however, can survive for a number of years. A harsh dictatorship can survive for some years on effectiveness alone, or even for decades if it maintains high effectiveness and some degree of legitimacy.[285]

Belarus remains a political anomaly and a *régime démodé* in the heart of Europe. It is the only country in the geographic borders of Europe that is not a member of the Council of Europe and, as a non-EU country, does not have the Partnership and Cooperation Agreement with the EU.

The current situation with human rights and civil society liberalization in Belarus is alarming. Lukashenka's regime is characterized by high autocratic resilience, which makes any politically deviant behavior punishable. Grzegorz Gromadzki *et al.* present quite gloomy prospects:

> In the future, we can expect to witness new repressions by Europe's last dictator and further deterioration of the situation. . . . Lukashenka will do everything in his power to oppress the political opposition, NGOs and the media in order to ensure the extension of his rule.

. . . [C]o-operation with Lukashenka's regime is and will be, for the foreseeable future, impossible.[286]

Under the present circumstances, the U.S. Government should continue working with Belarusian civil society both domestically and abroad[287] to increase its inputs in Belarusian political life.

The United States has had a very cautious but consistent policy with regards to Belarus. It has been a constant critic of the human rights violations and the impeding of the civil society development in Belarus. In 2004, the U.S. Congress adopted so-called "Belarus Democracy Act" committing:

[t]o assist the people of the Republic of Belarus in regaining their freedom and to enable them to join the European community of democracies; to encourage free and fair presidential, parliamentary, and local elections in Belarus, conducted in a manner consistent with internationally accepted standards and under the supervision of internationally recognized observers; To assist in restoring and strengthening institutions of democratic governance in Belarus.[288]

The biggest achievement of the Act, according to Stewart Parker, "was that the U.S. anti-Lukashenka rhetoric was given the 'legal base' that legitimized turning words into action."[289] Notwithstanding the baseline for support to the Belarusian civil society, U.S. assistance has been constantly decreasing, due to the strong and repressive grip on the domestic political life of the current regime.

Belarus is also the only country among the three discussed here that has experienced foreign political and economic punitive actions against it. In addition to supporting civil society development, the

U.S. Government, together with the EU, has been on and off imposing sanctions on Belarus demanding for the improvement of the domestic political situation, including the release of political prisoners and lifting the repressions against Belarusian civil society. The sanctions were applied in 2008 with a short relief in 2009–10 and then reinstated in 2011 as a response to the fraudulent elections. These sanctions embraced economic and political pressure on Belarusian leadership and several state-owned companies, including visa restrictions for Lukashenka and his close entourage.[290] The 2004 Act was reinforced by the 2012 Belarus Democracy and Human Rights Act, which envisaged further political containment of Lukashenka's regime.

With their comprehensive nature, the effectiveness of the sanctions imposed on Belarus is dubious. On the one hand, they show the U.S. attitude towards the regime. As the country vitally interested in promotion of democratic governance as the governing principle in the world, the United States cannot stay dormant to the systematic human rights violations and oppressions of the Belarusian citizens. On the other, these sanctions have little, if no, real influence on the domestic political or climate in Belarus, being back-up in both these spheres by its patron, Russia. The movement towards China is rather an attempt to gain short-term economic benefits than a real long-term project. Toughening of the sanctions would not bring the desired effect here: Belarus is highly Russia-oriented in its exports. Besides, the Belarusian companies, if needed, can trade with the rest of the world through the third-party subsidiaries in Russia, thus, bypassing trade restrictions.

There is also another fear "about Russian efforts to strengthen its sphere of influence in the region." By "isolating Belarus, the EU and United States are playing into Moscow's hands, without achieving real gains on democratization."[291] In such a specific political climate, a strategy that can bring the desired results should be somewhat similar to the *"congagement"*[292] policies — a mix of containment and engagement — as proposed by Zalmay Khalilzad in relation to Pakistan. The positive trait — if such a word can be applied to the current regime in Belarus — of Lukashenka, in comparison with the former communist rule, is absence of ideology-laden rivalry with the West, in general, and the United States, in particular. The congagement strategy applied toward the Belarusian government can lead to the desired policy outcome since not tinted by ideological burden Lukashenka's regime can become more pliable if offered more carrots than sticks.

Out of the three countries, Belarus is the least exposed to international military cooperation and partnership. As an economy, politics and culture, its main partner in the military field is Russia. As a Union State composed of Russia and Belarus, it has to protect its joint borders, which, in case of the latter, are directly facing the NATO. The Group of Belarus and Russian Forces is located in two strategic radars: the "Volga" radar in Hantsavichy operating on the basis of the Russian-Belarusian Military Agreement of 1995 and Baranovichi radar with 1,200 soldiers built in 2003 to substitute for the old Soviet radar in Skrunda (Latvia). Both radars are capable of detecting ballistic missiles in space at a distance of several thousand miles, identifying and evaluating those targets with their coordinates, and providing control over the western direction in azimuth range of 120 degrees.[293] Interesting enough, Russia is exempt from compensating the Belarus government for using those radars.

Currently, there are talks of Russia building the third military base—an air force regiment—by 2015 to protect the joint borders of the common state. This move, however, is received with low enthusiasm in the Belarusian opposition political establishment. According to Natalia Makushina:

> The Kremlin has long been using Lukashenka's desire to retain power at any cost with the purpose of promoting its projects in the former Soviet Union. The result of tactics 'after me, the deluge' of the Belarusian leader . . . has already led to serious problems in relations with the West. Chronic dependence on Russian preferences . . . is dangerous because it deprives Belarus of the opportunity to make its own political decisions, including in the military sphere.[294]

Indeed, the closer Belarus is to Russia, the farther away it moves from the bilateral and multilateral cooperation in the military sphere with the West.

Partnership with the NATO structures is limited to participation of Belarus in the PfP exercise starting from 1995. For this endeavor, Belarus has reserved a peacekeeping battalion, a military police platoon, 15 officers in the multinational headquarters, military transport aircraft Il-76MD, seven doctors, a mobile hospital, and a multifunctional nuclear, biological, and chemical (NBC) platoon.[295] Belarus is absent in any other participation in multidimensional and multilateral peacekeeping operation led by the Western countries. The minimalist approach is based on the nature of the political climate in the country where the Euro-Atlantic structures is still viewed largely within the confrontational context. There is no current co-operation between the United States and Belarusian military institutions. The point to keep in mind is that any future interaction will be contingent upon Lukashenka's will. It will serve his personal preference and will be presented domestically with the sole purpose of increasing his own political stakes.

The Eastern direction of Belarusian military cooperation, on the other hand, has recently been rigorously explored. In particular, Belarus is involved in close military partnership with China in the sphere of joint production of high-precision weapons; electronic warfare; air defense systems, and multiwheeled chassis and tractors for special installation. An example of the partnership is the Belarusian-Chinese joint venture "Minsk Wheel Tractor Plant (MWTP)" with the Belarusian share of 30 percent and the Chinese "Aerospace Corporation "Sanjiang" holding the remaining 70 percent.[296] According to some experts, China, under the NATO military embargo imposed after the Tiananmen events of 1989, is keen to obtain the latest military technologies, and Belarus turned to be a ready supplier.

CONCLUSIONS

The findings of the research expand on the null hypothesis of the negative influence of democracy over the political stability and economic development of Ukraine, Georgia, and Belarus. They also largely substantiate the thesis on the role autocratic resilience, economic development, and third-party interest play in mitigating or aggravating threats to internal and external stability. The results of the public opinion polls and face-to-face interviews with the key stakeholders show that in the countries with developing political cultures, political stability and economic development depend on the authoritarian resilience and economic support from abroad (Belarus). In absence of these conditions under increasing globalization, the countries had to mimic the existing democratic practices, which under the influence of unsettled political cultures reveal the breach between the outputs and inputs of the political process. They adopt democratic practices without proper institutional socialization (Georgia and Ukraine), which leads to high political instability and low social and economic development.

In countries at the early stages of their independence, the choice for democracy, paradoxically, brought more political instability than for authoritarian governance. The character of political interactions in any country is determined by the procedure of transfer of power (which is a form of public inputs in the governance process). The wider population circles are involved in the governance processes, the more dynamic the power transience becomes. In democracies, it is achieved by means of established effective norms, rules, and standards, which jointly allow for peaceful domestic political processes. To keep political stability in these societies, democracies require highly developed political cultures, which would permit the expressions of free will within the democratically accepted frameworks of policymaking. At the same time, democracy is one of the least punitive regimes— generally speaking and with reference to the core of democratic governance as extended to the large circles of citizens. Popular discontent with policies is accommodated through mechanisms of political participation, rule of law, and democratic governance rather than direct suppression of political deviance.

In stark contrast to it is the autocratic rule, which stifles most of the signs of deviation with its punitive policies. The political process here is static, and with the high costs of entry into the political lives of new actors, even more so for those disassociated with the ruling regimes. The process of power transfer happens either within the close circles of supporters of the regime or only after the removal of the autocrat from governance. As a result, all the autocracies need to keep their domestic stability is the constant iron fist of effective punishment for political deviation and the good health of an autocrat. Appearance of any dictator, like Lukashenka, inevitably leads to the test of political durability of the regime.

From the point of view of power transience and the domestic political process, Georgia is the most democratic and vibrant, followed by Ukraine. Political stability in Georgia depends on the ability of the institutional actors to act within the democratic frameworks. Power transience, by definition, is not a negative process; it is a sign of a healthy domestic polity. It starts negatively affecting the political stability if undertaken outside of the democratic frameworks and disregards the rules of democratic institutional design. Belarus, on its part, is the most politically static but, nevertheless, is a very stable country. By restricting public participation, the government keeps the monopoly over political processes and forcefully prevents the expressions of dissatisfaction with its actions.

In more advanced democracies, democratic governance, on the contrary, contributes to the internal and external political stability by operating democratic institutions effectively. Via open and free participation of all layers of the society in the political processes, democracies limit the chances for unexpected and, mostly, forceful governmental changes and provide for the political longevity of democratic institutions. Construction of a democratic political system is a necessary condition for the development of national institutions outside the political culture. When they are absent or weak, the system is stable, but there is no basis for democracy. When they are present, they become destabilizing factors, but they ensure the preservation of a competitive political system.

In trying to accelerate the process of building democratic institutions, a newly created country has the only option available for it: to accept, or "mimic," the existing structures and agencies of the advanced democracies and to try to adapt them to their own political environs. In Georgia, due to its open and widely tolerant political culture, the regime mimicry is almost full; what is lacking is the final stage of the democratic institutionalization: norm internalization. The undetermined and ambiguous political culture in Ukraine makes mimicry partial—well developed in some spheres, while lacking in others. The dormant and suppressed political culture of Belarus had halted the mimicry in the embryonic stage, where there are some institutions that resemble those in advanced democracies, but they utterly lack socialization among the institutional actors.

In order to be successful and contribute to long-lasting political stability, democracy should be "lived through"; it should be the paramount of the political evolutionary process. If offered from outside, the success of the democratization process would depend on the rigidity of political culture, internally, and the interest of third parties, externally. The United States has been assisting Ukraine, Georgia, and Belarus on their different paths to democratic governance. This support, however diverse and multifaceted, is directed towards keeping these countries politically stable, economically developed and socially self-sustainable. While Georgia and, to a certain degree, Ukraine are firmly committed to democratic development, Belarus remains a clear outlier with its autocratic leadership. However, there is hope that the society will eventually wake up from the 2 decades of lethargy and take back the powers that belong to them. Ultimately, it is up to the people themselves to decide which governance regime "fits" them better. All they have to do is to prove to the generations to come that their initial decisions to follow the democratic designs were not accidental, but the carefully planned and experienced results of historical choices they made.

ENDNOTES

1. Gretchen Helmke and Steven Levitski, *Informal Institutions and Democracy. Lessons from Latin America*, Baltimore, MD: The Johns Hopkins University Press, 2006, p. 6.

2. Yi Feng, "Democracy, Political Stability and Economic Growth," *British Journal of Political Science*, Vol. 27, No. 3, 1997, p. 441.

3. *Ibid.*, p. 398.

4. Krister Lundell, "Autocratic Stability and Democratization: The Impact of Political Economy and Governance," Paper prepared for the panel, "Bad Guys, Good Governance? Varieties of Capitalism in Autocracies," at the International Political Science Association - European Consortium of Political Research (IPSA-ECPR) Joint Conference, 2012.

5. Susanna Lundström, "Decomposed Effects of Democracy on Economic Freedom," Working Paper in *Economics*, Vol. 74, 2002, Göteborg University, Sweden, p. 16.

6. Rogers Brubaker, "Nationhood and National Question in the Soviet Union and Post-Soviet Eurasia: An Institutional Account," *Theory and Society*, Vol. 23, 1994, pp. 55-76.

7. Erin K. Jenne, "A Bargaining Theory of Minority Demands: Explaining the Dog that Didn't Bite in 1990 Yugoslavia," *International Studies Quarterly*, Vol. 48, 2004, pp. 729-754.

8. Robert Nalbandov, *Foreign Interventions in Ethnic Conflicts*, Farnham, UK: Ashgate Publishing, 2009.

9. A. J. Nathan, "China's Changing of the Guard: Authoritarian Resilience," *Journal of Democracy*, Vol. 14, 2003, pp. 6–17.

10. Eurasia Group, *Global Political Risk Index*, New York: Institute for Economics and Peace, 2010.

11. Claude Ake, "A Definition of Political Stability," *Comparative Politics*, Vol. 7, No. 2, January 1975, p. 273.

12. Ahmed Samatar, "Somalia: Statelessness as Homelessness," Ahmed Samatar and Abdi Samatar, eds., *The African State. Reconsiderations*, Portsmouth, NH: Heinemann, 2002, p. 12.

13. Mohamed Sahnoun, *Somalia. The Missed Opportunities*, Washington, DC: United States Institute of Peace, 1994, p. 28.

14. *Global Peace Index 2011*, New York: Institute for Economics and Peace, 2011, p. 40.

15. Seymour Martin Lipset, "Some Social Requisites of Democracy: Economic Development and Political Legitimacy," *The American Political Science Review*, Vol. 53, No. 1, March 1959, p. 86.

16. *Ibid.*

17. Jack A. Goldstone, "Pathways to State Failure," *Conflict Management and Peace Science*, Vol. 25, 2008, p. 285.

18. Ben Shepherd, "Political Stability: Crucial for Growth?" *IDEAS Report, SU004 – Resurgent Continent? Africa and the World*, 2010, p. 9.

19. Yi Feng, "Democracy, Political Stability, and Economic Growth," p. 398.

20. Lisa Chauvet, Paul Collier, and Anke Hoeffler, "The Cost of Failing States and the Limits to Sovereignty," paper prepared for WIDER, February 2007, p. 3.

21. Cecilia Emma Sottilotta, "Political Stability in Authoritarian Regimes: Lessons from the Arab Uprisings," working paper prepared for *Instituto Affari Internazionali*, Vol. 1301, 2013, p. 2.

22. Plato, *Crito*, London, UK: Book Jungle, 2008.

23. John Locke, *Second Treatise of Government*, Charleston, SC: CreateSpace, 2013, p. 3.

24. Lipset, "Some Social Requisites of Democracy: Economic Development and Political Legitimacy," pp. 86–87.

25. Aaron Wildavsky, "Choosing Preferences by Constructing Institutions: A Cultural Theory of Preference Formation," *American Political Science Review*, Vol. 81, 1987, p. 6.

26. Charles T. Call, "Beyond the 'Failed State': Toward Conceptual Alternatives," *European Journal of International Relations*, Vol. 17, No. 1, 2010, p. 308.

27. Both this quote and the one preceding it can be found in Thomas Hobbes, *Leviathan*, Huntington, WV: Empire Books, 2013.

28. Vital Silitski, "From Social Contract to Social Dialogue: Some Observations on the Nature and Dynamics of Social Contracting in Modern Belarus," Kiryl Haiduk, Elena Rakova, and Vital Silitski, eds., *Social Contracts in Contemporary Belarus*, Minsk: Belarusian Institute for Strategic Studies, 2009, p. 156.

29. Kiryl Haiduk, "Social Contract: a Conceptual Framework" in Kiryl Haiduk, Elena Rakova, Vital Silitski, eds., *Social Contracts in Contemporary Belarus*, Minsk, Belarus: Belarusian Institute for Strategic Studies, 2009, p. 22.

30. A. J. Nathan, "China's Changing of the Guard: Authoritarian Resilience," *Journal of Democracy*, Vol. 14, 2003, pp. 6–17.

31. Adam Przeworski and Fernando Limongi, "Political Regimes and Economic Growth," *The Journal of Economic Perspectives*, Vol. 7, No. 3, 1993, p. 58.

32. Immanuel Kant, *Perpetual Peace and Other Essays on Politics, History and Morals*, Ted Humphrey, trans., Indianapolis, IN/ Cambridge, MA: Hacket Publishing Company, 1983, p. 112.

33. John R. Oneal and Bruce Russett, "The Kantian Peace: The Pacific Benefits of Democracy, Interdependence, and International Organizations, 1885-1992," *World Politics*, Vol. 52, No. 1, 1999, pp. 1–37.

34. Kant, *Perpetual Peace and Other Essays on Politics, History, and Morals*, p. 109.

35. Adam Smith, *The Wealth of Nations*, Blacksburg, VA: Thrifty Books, 2009.

36. Lipset, "Some Social Requisites of Democracy: Economic Development and Political Legitimacy," p. 75.

37. Lundell, "Autocratic Stability and Democratization."

38. Milton Friedman, *Capitalism and Freedom*, Chicago, IL: University of Chicago Press, 1962.

39. Yi Feng, "Democracy, Political Stability and Economic Growth," p. 393.

40. Przeworski and Limongi, "Political Regimes and Economic Growth," p. 51.

41. *Ibid.*, p. 54.

42. Edward D. Mansfield, Helen V. Milner, and B. Peter Rosendorff, "Free to Trade: Democracies, Autocracies, and International Trade," *The American Political Science Review*, Vol. 94, No. 2, June 2000, p. 318.

43. Przeworski and Limongi, pp. 51–69.

44. John Maynard Keynes, *The General Theory Of Employment, Interest, And Money*, New York: Prometeus Books, Reprint Edition, 1997.

45. *Freedom in The World 2013*, Washington, DC; Freedom House, 2013, p. 4.

46. Monty G. Marshall and Keith Jaggers, "Polity IV Project: Political Regime Characteristics and Transitions, 1800–2002," Integrated Network for Societal Conflict Research Program, College Park, MD: Center for International Development and Conflict Management, University of Maryland, 2012.

47. *Press Freedom Index 2013*, Paris, France: Reporters without Borders, 2013.

48. D. Kaufmann, A. Kraay, and M. Mastruzzi, "The World-wide Governance Indicators: Methodology and Analytical Issues," *World Bank Policy Research Working Paper* No. 5430, Washington, DC: The World Bank, 2010.

49. *Ibid*.

50. "Sociological Poll," Kyiv, Ukraine: The Razumkov Center, July 20–28, 2009, available from *www.razumkov.org.ua/eng/poll.php?poll_id=516*.

51. "Transparency International," *Transparency International*, available from *gcb.transparency.org/gcb201011/results/*.

52. "The World Development Indicators," *Development Data Group*, Washington, DC: The World Bank, 2012.

53. "2013 Index of Economic Freedom," Washington, DC: The Heritage Foundation, 2013, available from *www.heritage.org/index/*.

54. "Doing Business. Measuring Business Regulations: Economy Rankings," Washington, DC: International Financial Corporation, 2012, available from *www.doingbusiness.org/rankings*.

55. "GEORGIA: Partial progress towards durable solutions for IDPs," Geneva, Switzerland: Internal Displacement Monitoring Center, 2012.

56. Axel Dreher, Noel Gaston, and Pim Martens, *Measuring Globalization – Gauging its Consequence*, New York: Springer, 2008.

57. "Sto Dollarov s Nosa Plati i Ezjai Zagranicu" ("Pay 100 dollars and Go Abroad"), *GazeraRu*, September 7, 2013, available from *www.gazeta.ru/social/2013/09/07/5642365.shtml*.

58. *The Failed States Index 2013*.

59. Monty G. Marshall and Benjamin R. Cole, "Polity IV Project: Political Regime Characteristics and Transitions, 1800–2012," *Global Report 2011: Conflict, Governance and State Fragility*, Integrated Network for Societal Conflict Research Program, College Park, MD: Center for International Development and Conflict Management, University of Maryland, 2011.

60. EUROSTAT 2012, Luxembourg, 2012.

61. Roy Walmsey, *World Prison Population List*, 9th Ed, London, UK: International Centre for Prison Studies, 2011.

62. *Global Peace Index 2013*, New York: Institute for Economics and Peace, 2013, p. 13.

63. *Ibid*, p. 12.

64. "Political Stability Index 2009–2010," *Economist Intelligence Unit*, London, UK, available from *viewswire.eiu.com/site_info. asp?info_name=social_unrest_table&page=noads*.

65. D. Kaufmann, A. Kraay, and M. Mastruzzi, "The Worldwide Governance Indicators: Methodology and Analytical Issues," *World Bank Policy Research Working Paper* No. 5430, Washington, DC: The World Bank, 2010.

66. Axel Dreher, Noel Gaston, and Pim Martens, *Measuring Globalization – Gauging its Consequence*, New York: Springer, 2008.

67. The latest round of the diplomatic quarrel was the expelling of the Swedish and Polish ambassadors from Belarus over the extension of the sanctions against Lukashenka's regime, with the most notable case being the deportation of U.S. Ambassador Karen Stewart in 2008.

68. *Democracy Assessment: The Basics of International IDEA Assessment Framework*, Stockholm, Sweden: International Institute of Democracy and Electoral Assistance, available from *www.idea.int/ publications/sod/upload/demo_ass_inlay_eng_L.pdf*.

69. "Guide to Rule of Law. Country Analyses: The Rule of Law Strategic Framework." *A Guide for the USAID Democracy and Governance Officers*, Washington, DC: United States Agency for International Development, January 2010.

70. Douglas North, *Institutions, Institutional Change and Economic Performance*, Cambridge, UK: Cambridge University Press, 1990, p. 37.

71. Lowell Dittmer, "Political Culture and Political Symbolism: Toward a Theoretical Synthesis," *World Politics*, Vol. 29, 1977, p. 566.

72. Claude Ake, "A Definition of Political Stability," *Comparative Politics*, Vol. 7, No. 2, 1975, p. 271.

73. David D. Laitin and Aaron Wildavsky. "Political Culture and Political Preferences," *The American Political Science Review*, Vol. 82, No. 2, June 1988, p. 589.

74. Stephen Chilton, "Defining Political Culture." *The Western Political Quarterly*, Vol. 41, No. 3, 1988, p. 431.

75. Martha Finnemore and Kathryn Sikkink, "International Norm Dynamics and Political Change," *International Organizations*, Vol. 52, No. 4, 1998, p. 896.

76. Sergei Shtukarin, "Ukrainian Identity Matrix," Donetsk Oblast, Ukraine: Center for Political Studies Non-Paper, Donetsk National University, June 25, 2013.

77. Serhy Yekelchuk, *Ukraine: Birth of a Modern Nation*, New York: Oxford University Press, 2007, p. 5.

78. Orest Subtelny, *Ukraine. A History*, 4th Ed., Toronto, Canada: University of Toronto Press, 2009, pp. 19–41.

79. Anna Reid, *Borderland. A Journey through the History of Ukraine*, Boulder, CO: Basic Books, 2000, p. 1.

80. Stefan Tomashivsky, *Istoriya Ukrainy: Starynni viku i seredni viku, (History of Ukraine: Ancient Times and Middle Ages)*, Munich, Germany: UVU, 1948.

81. Paul Robert Magocsi, *A History of Ukraine. The Land and Its People*, Toronto, Canada: University of Toronto Press, 2010, pp. 133–143.

82. Anders Aslund, *How Ukraine Became a Market Economy and Democracy*, Washington, DC: Peterson Institute for International Economics, 2009, p. 11.

83. Omeljan Pritsak, "The First Constitution of Ukraine, 5 April 1750," Cultures and Nations of Central and Eastern Europe, *Harvard Ukrainian Studies*, Vol. 22, 1998, pp. 471–496.

84. William Penn Cresson. *The Cossacks: Their History and Country*, Norwood, MA: The Pimpton Press, 1919.

85. Glenn E. Curtis, *Armenia, Azerbaijan, and Georgia: Country Studies,* Charleston, SC: CreateSpace, 2013, p. 157.

86. N. A. Berdzenishvili, V. D. Dondua, M. K. Dumbadze, G. A. Melikishvili, and Sh. A. Meskhia, *Istoriya Gruzii. S Drevneishix Vremen Do 60-x Godov XIX Veka (History of Georgia: From the Ancient Times to 1860s)*, Tbilisi, Georgia: State Publishing House of the Educational-Pedagogical Literature, 1962.

87. Donald Rayfield, *Edge of Empires. A History of Georgia*, London, UK: Reaktion Books Ltd., 2012, p. 250.

88. W. E. D. Allen, "The New Political Boundaries in the Caucasus," *The Geographic Journal*, Vol. 69, No. 5, 1927, p. 431.

89. Jan Zaprudnik, *Balarus: At a Crossroads of History*, Boulder, CO: Westview Press, 1993, p. 2.

90. *Ibid.*, pp. 10–20.

91. Andrew Wilson, *Belarus: The Last European Dictatorship*, New Haven, CT: Yale University Press, 2011, p. 59.

92. Serhii Plokhy, *The Origins of the Slavic Nations: Modern Identities in Russia, Ukraine, and Belarus*, Cambridge, UK: Cambridge University Press, 2010, pp. 360–361.

93. M. Krajhanovski, "Крыжаноўскі М. Жывая крыніца ты, родная мова" ("Living Source You Are, My Native Tongue"), *Narodnaya Volya*, 2008, pp. 65–66.

94. David R. Marples, *Belarus: From Soviet Rule to Nuclear Catastrophe*, Basingstoke, UK: Palgrave Macmillan, 1996, p. 4.

95. Joseph Stalin, *Sochineniya*, Vol. 12, Moscow, Russia: State Publishing House of Political Literature, 1949, p. 369.

96. Wilson, *Belarus: The Last European Dictatorship*, p. 124.

97. J. W. R. Parsons, "National Integration in Soviet Georgia," *Soviet Studies*, Vol. 34, No. 4, 1982, p. 548.

98. Anna Reid, *Borderland. A Journey Through The History of Ukraine*, Boulder, CO: Basic Books, 2000, p. 64.

99. Chaim Kaufman, "Possible and Impossible Solutions to Ethnic Civil War," Michael Brown *et al.*, eds., *Nationalism and Ethnic Conflict*, Cambridge, MA: MIT Press, 1997, p. 274.

100. According to Pavel Stephanovski, Stalin "hated the Georgian intelligentsia as the class enemy" and ordered Beria to lead the execution squads to eliminate the Georgian elite in 1924. See Pavel Stephanovski, "Развороты Судьбы: Автобиографическая Повесть" ("Cross-Roads of Fate: An Autobiography"), *RUDN*, 200201502003, available from *www.sakharov-center.ru/asfcd/auth/?t=page&num=9748*.

101. Zbigniew Brzezinski, "The Premature Partnership?" *Foreign Affairs*, Vol. 73, No. 2, 1994, p. 80.

102. Robert Conquest, *The Harvest of Sorrow: Soviet Collectivization and the Terror-Famine*, Oxford, UK: Oxford University Press, 1986, p. 4.

103. S. Kulchytsky, "Террор Голодомор Как Инструмент Коллективизации" ("Terror-Famine as an Instrument of Collectivization"), *Terror-Famine 1932-1933 in Ukraine: Causes and Consequence* (Holodomor 1932-1933 rr. V Ukraini: prychyny i naslydki), Kyiv, Ukraine: Institut Istorii Ukrainiy NANU, 1995, p. 34.

104. Miron Dolot, *Execution by Hunger: The Hidden Holocaust*, New York: W. W. Norton & Company, 1987.

105. Lundell, "Autocratic Stability and Democratization."

106. Anders, Aslund, and Michael McFaul, *Revolution in Orange. The Origins of Ukraine's Democratic Breakthrough*, Washington, DC: Carnegie Endowment of International Peace, 2006, p. 29.

107. Aslund, *How Ukraine Became a Market Economy and Democracy*, p. 32.

108. *Ibid.*, pp. 43–56.

109. *Ibid.*, p. 75.

110. "Початок Економічних Реформ" ("Beginning of Economic Reforms"), *History of Ukraine*, available from *histua.com/knigi/konspekt-lekcij-z-istoriya-ukraini/pochatok-ekonomichnix-reform*.

111. Wilson, *Ukraine's Orange Revolution*, pp. 53–54.

112. Lucan A. Way, "Ukraine's Orange Revolution. Kuchma's Failed Authoritarianism," *Journal of Democracy*, Vol. 16, No. 2, 2005, p. 131.

113. Aslund and McFaul, p. 39.

114. P. J. D'Anieri, *Orange Revolution and Aftermath: Mobilization, Apathy, and the State in Ukraine*, Baltimore, MD: The Johns Hopkins University Press, 2010.

115. Alexander Suzdalcev, quoted in Rustem Falyakhov, Jana Milyukova, and Constantine Shiyan, "Украине Не Дают Добро"("No Green Light for Ukraine"), *GazetaRU,* August 14, 2013, available from *www.gazeta.ru/business/2013/08/14/5566285.shtml.*

116. "U.S. Overseas Loans and Grants," Washington, DC: United States Agency for International Development (USAID), 2011, country files available from *gbk.eads.usaidallnet.gov.*

117. Steven Woehrel, "Ukraine: Current Issues and U.S. Policy, May 24, 2013," *Congressional Research Service Report* 7-5700, RL33460, Washington, DC: Congressional Research Service, 2013.

118. "European Union provides €30 million for institutional reforms in Ukraine," European Commission Press Release, IP/11/881, Brussels, Belgium: European Union, July 13, 2011.

119. Per Gahrton, *Georgia: Pawn in the New Great Game*, New York: Pluto Press, 2010, p. 81.

120. Eduard Shevardandze's speech at the 25th Congress of the Georgian Communist Party, 1983, quoted in Bohdan Nahaylo and Victor Swoboda, *Soviet Disunion: A History of the Nationalities Problem in the USSR*, London, UK: Hamish Hamilton, 2010, p. 189.

121. "Georgia-NATO: Friends Forever," *Newsagency Utro*, September 26, 2000, available from *www.utro.ru/articles/politics/2000/09/26/200009260332183024.shtml?2000/09/26.*

122. Jonathan Wheatley, *Georgia from National Awakening to Rose Revolution: Delayed Transition in the Former Soviet Union*, Aldershot, UK: Ashgate Publishing, 2005, p. 104.

123. Rob Parsons, "Unrest Rises in Georgia," *Sunday Herald*, November 14, 2003.

124. B. Copieters and R. Legvold, eds., *Statehood and Security: Georgia after the Rose Revolution*, Cambridge, MA: The MIT Press, 2005.

125. Linkoln A. Mitchell, *Uncertain Democracy: U.S. Foreign Policy and Georgia's Rose Revolution*, Philadelphia, PA: University of Pennsylvania Press, 2008, p. 4.

126. Jim Nichol, *Georgia [Republic]: Recent Developments and U.S. Interests*, Washington, DC: Congressional Research Service, July 13, 2012.

127. R. Nalbandov, "Battle of Two Logics: Appropriateness and Consequentiality in Russian Interventions in Georgia," *Caucasian Review of International Affairs*, Vol. 3, No. 1, 2009, pp. 20–35.

128. Several times, Lukashenka made the statement, "Belarus is the same Russian but with a quality mark," quoted in Roy Medvedev, Александр Лукашенко: Контуры Беларуской Модели (*Alexander Lukashenka: Contours of the Belarusian Model*), Moscow, Russia: BBPG: ЗАО "ББПГ," 2010.

129. Andrew Savchenko, *Belarus – A Perpetual Borderland*, Leiden, The Netherlands: Brill Academic Pub, 2009, p. 179.

130. Alexander Feduta, *Lukashenka: Politicheskay Biografiya*, (*Lukashenka: Political Bio*), Moscow, Russia: Referendum, 2005, p. 205.

131. Steven Levistki and Lucan A. Way, *Competitive Authoritarianism: Hybrid Regimes After the Cold War*, Cambridge, UK: Cambridge University Press, 2010, p. 204.

132. Juri Cavusau, "Belarus' Civic Sector," Pejda, ed., *Hopes, Illusions, Perspectives: Belarusian Society*, Warsaw, Poland-Minsk, Belarus: East European Democratic Centre, 2007, p. 9.

133. A. Gura, "Нам Есть Что Защищать" ("We Have Things To Protect"), *Belarusskaya Dumka*, Vol. 5, pp. 31–42, available from *beldumka.belta.by/isfiles/000167_673383.pdf.*

134. Brian Bennett. *The Last Dictatorship in Europe: Belarus Under Lukashenko*, New York: Columbia University Press, p. 20.

135. Petr Kravchenko, quoted in Feduta, p. 65.

136. *Foreign Operations Appropriated Assistance: Belarus*, Washington, DC: U.S. Department of State, Bureau of European and Eurasian Affairs, April, 2008, available from *2001-2009.state.gov/p/eur/rls/fs/107776.htm#graphs*.

137. Steven Woehrel, *Belarus: Background and U.S. Policy Concerns*, Washington, DC: Congressional Research Service, February 2013.

138. "European Commission Confirms Strong Support to the Belarusian Population," European Commission, IP/10/330, Brussels, Belgium: European Union, March 2011.

139. Gordon Fairclough, "Belarus Opposition Gets Aid," *The Wall Street Journal*, February 3, 2011.

140. Askold Krushnelnycky, *An Orange Revolution: A Personal Journey Through Ukrainian History*, London, UK: Secker & Warburg, 2006, p. 78.

141. *Sociological Poll*, Kyiv, Ukraine: Razumkov Center, available from *www.razumkov.org.ua/eng/poll.php?poll_id=211*.

142. *Ibid.*

143. *Human Rights Watch Report 2013*, p. 500.

144. *Freedom in the World 2013*, Washington, DC: Freedom House, 2013, p. 7.

145. *Sociology Poll*, "If next elections to the Verkhovna Rada of Ukraine were held today, which party or electoral bloc would you vote for?" Kyiv, Ukraine: Razumkov Center, April 12–16, 2013.

146. "Klichko: There Should Be a Single Candidate from the Opposition," *GazetaRU*, August 8, 2013, available from *www.gazeta.ru/politics/news/2013/08/20/n_3125301.shtml*.

147. Victoria Sumar, "'Stage 'Start' Or 'There Are Only Three of Them Left', Etap "Start" abo "Ikh Lishilos Troe," *Ukrainskaya Pravda*, July 4, 2013, available from *www.pravda.com.ua/articles/2013/07/4/6993401/*.

148. The Razumkov Center, "The Middle Class as the Prerequisite for Ukraine's Democratic Future," *National Security and Defense*, No. 7, 2008, p. 2.

149. *Ibid.*, p. 4.

150. "Torgovo-Ekonomicheskoe Sotrudnichestvo Ukraini I Rossiii" ("Trade-Economic Cooperation Between Ukraine and Russia"), Embassy of Ukraine in the Russian Federation, 2012, available from *russia.mfa.gov.ua/ru/ukraine-ru/trade*.

151. Boris Heifetz, "Rossiya-Ukraina. Neformalnaya Integraciya" ("Russia-Ukraine. An Informal Integration"), *Mirovaya Ekonomika, Pryamie Investicii (World Economy, Direct Investments)*, No. 2, 2013, p. 28.

152. "Rossiyane Kupyat Tri Nikolaevskix Sudostroitelnix Zavoda I Zaru-Mashproekt" ("The Russians Will Buy Three Shipyards in Nikolayev in Addition to Zarya-Mashproekt"), *NikVesi*, July 12, 2013, available from *www.nikvesti.com/news/11829*.

153. "Sociological Poll: Is Ukraine a European country?" Kyiv, Ukraine: The Razumkov Center, available from *www.razumkov.org.ua/eng/poll.php?poll_id=673*.

154. Sociological Poll, "Do you consider yourself to be European, to belong to the culture and the history of European community?" (regional distribution, age distribution) Kyiv, Ukraine: The Razumkov Center, available from *www.razumkov.org.ua/eng/poll.php?poll_id=672*.

155. "Azarov Prodoljit Balansirovat Mejdu ES I Tamojennim Soyuzom" ("Azarov Continues to Balance Between the EU and the Customs Union"), *DeloUA*, September 18, 2013.

156. Rustem Falyakhov, Jana Milyukova, and Constantine Shiyan, "Ukraine Ne Daut Dobro," *GazetaRU,* August 14, 2013, available from *www.gazeta.ru/business/2013/08/14/5566285.shtml.*

157. Mykola Sungurovskiy, "Ukraine-NATO: Expectations and Results," *National Security And Defense,* No. 9, 2006, p. 5.

158. Sociological Poll, "Do you support NATO's Enlargement to the East?" Kyiv, Ukraine: The Razumkov Center, available from *www.razumkov.org.ua/eng/poll.php?poll_id=751.*

159. Sociological Poll, "How should Ukraine act towards NATO?" Kyiv, Ukraine: The Razumkov Center, available from *www.razumkov.org.ua/eng/poll.php?poll_id=726.*

160. Sociological Poll "How would you vote if the referendum on Ukraine`s NATO accession was held the following Sunday?" 2002-2009, July 20-28, 2009, Kyiv, Ukraine: The Razumkov Center, available from *www.razumkov.org.ua/eng/poll.php?poll_id=46.*

161. Pavel Haydutskii, "Украина и Таможенный Союз: Проблемы Интеграции" ("Ukraine and the Customs Union: Problems of Integration"), March 26, 2013, available from *zn.ua/columnists/ukraina-i-tamozhennyy-soyuz-problemy-integracii-119431_.html.*

162. Mykola Riabchuk, "What's Left of Orange Ukraine?" *Eurozine,* March 2013, available from *www.eurozine.com/articles/2010-03-04-riabchuk-en.html.*

163. *Human Rights Watch Report 2013,* p. 441.

164. *Freedom in the World 2013,* p. 2.

165. Geoffrey M. Hodgson, "What Are Institutions," *Journal of Economic Issues,* Vol. XL, No. 1, 2006, p. 2.

166. Douglass C. North, "Institutions," *The Journal of Economic Perspectives,* Vol. 5, No. 1, 1991, p. 97.

167. Luis Navarro and Ian T. Woodward, *Public Attitudes in Georgia,* "Results of a February 2012 Survey," National Democratic Institute, Tbilisi, Georgia.

168. Lundell, "Autocratic Stability and Democratization."

169. Navarro and Woodward.

170. *Nations in Transit 2012, Georgia Report,* Washington, DC: Freedom House, 2012.

171. Anders Fogh Rasmussen, "NATO and Georgia — On the Right Path," Keynote speech at the National Library of Georgia, Tbilisi, Georgia, June 27, 2013.

172. "EU, Georgia Making 'Good Progress' in Association Agreement, Visa Liberalization Talks," CivilGe, September 3, 2012, available from *www.civil.ge/eng/article.php?id=25175.*

173. Balazs Jarabik and Alastair Rabagliati, "Assessing Democracy Assistance: Belarus," *FRIDE,* May 2010, p. 2

174. *World Report 2013, Human Rights Watch Report 2013,* p. 408.

175. Wilson, *Belarus: The Last European Dictatorship,* p. 191.

176. "Belarusians Wear Jeans in Silent Protest," *ABC News,* January 13, 2006, available from *abcnews.go.com/International/story?id=1502762#.UeDUjRbV1uI.*

177. "Belarus Opposition Leader Jailed," *BBC News,* July 14, 2006, available from *news.bbc.co.uk/2/hi/europe/5178714.stm.*

178. "Belarus: 7 Presidential Candidates Face 15 Years," *Kyiv-Post,* December 22, 2010, available from *www.kyivpost.com/content/russia-and-former-soviet-union/belarus-7-presidential-candidates-face-15-years-93334.html.*

179. Michael Schwirtz, "Clashes in Belarus Show Resilience of Both Sides," *The New York Times,* December 21, 2010, available from *www.nytimes.com/2010/12/22/world/europe/22belarus.html?_r=0.*

180. Jerome Taylor, "In Europe's Last Dictatorship, All Opposition is Mercilessly Crushed," *The Independent*, March 2010, available from *www.independent.co.uk/news/world/europe/in-europes-last-dictatorship-all-opposition-is-mercilessly-crushed-2235153.html*.

181. "Belarus: Lukashenka vows to quell 'revolution plot.'" *BBC News Europe*, July 2, 2011, available from *www.bbc.co.uk/news/world-europe-14006365*.

182. *Freedom in the World 2013*, p. 2.

183. "Social Situation in Belarus in 2009," Minsk, Belarus: Belarus Institute of Strategic Studies, 2010.

184. *World Report 2013, Human Rights Watch Report 2013*, p. 405.

185. "Оппозиционный Авитаминоз" ("Oppositional Avitaminosiss"), Brighton, UK: Independent Institute for Social-Economic and Political Studies, March 1, 2013, available from *www.iiseps.org/analitica/540*.

186. "Какая Власть Нужна Белорусам" ("What Power The Belarusians Need"), Brighton, UK: Independent Institute for Social-Economic and Political Studies, March 1, 2013, available from *www.iiseps.org/analitica/541*.

187. "Сердце Царя—Лучшая Конституция?" ("King's Heart—Best Constitution?"), March 1, 2013, available from *www.iiseps.org/analitica/542*.

188. Intelligence Unit, *Index of Democracy 2011, The Economist*, p. 21.

189. Steven Levistki and Lucan A. Way, *Competitive Authoritarianism: Hybrid Regimes After the Cold War*, Cambridge, UK: Cambridge University Press, 2010, p. 186.

190. Feduta, p. 418.

191. Interview with Tamara Vikkikova, former head of the Belarusian National Bank and exiled in Great Britain, *Komersant*, No. 158/П, 2288, March 9, 2001, available from *www.kommersant.ru/doc/281285?fp=*.

192. Charter 97, "Сенсационный Фильм О Лукашенко на НТВ, Полная Версия Видео" ("Sensational Movie on Lukashenka: Uncut Version"), July 4, 2010, available from *charter97.org/ru/news/2010/7/4/30348/*.

193. Newsland, "Белорусский ТВ канал обозвал Путина "дураком" ("Belarusian TV Channel Called Putin 'A fool',"), September 3, 2010, available from *newsland.com/news/detail/id/553972/*.

194. "Содействие инвестициям" ("Facilitation of Investments"), Minsk, Belarus: Ministry of Foreign Affairs of Belarus, available from *www.mfa.gov.by/investments/*.

195. "В 2012 году иностранные инвестиции в Беларуси сократились на 25%" ("In 2012 Foreign Investments in Belarus Decreased by 25%"), *TelegrafBY*.

196. "Поток Иностранных Инвестиций в Беларусь Заметно Уменьшился" ("Foreign Investments in Belarus Drastically Decreased"), *TUT.BY*, February 2, 2013, available from *news.tut.by/economics/333001.html*.

197. "Российские Инвестиции в Беларусь в 2009 Году Увеличились в 2,8 Раза" ("Russian Investments in Belarus In 2009 Increased 2.8 times"), *TUT.BY*, March 18, 2010, available from *news.tut.by/economics/164391.html*.

198. "По Объемам Накопленных Российских Инвестиций Беларусь Опережает Австрию и Германию" ("By the Volumes of the Russian Investments, Belarus is Far Ahead of Austria and Germany"), *Ejednevnik*, November 23, 2011, available from *www.ej.by/news/economy/2011/11/23/po_ob_emam_nakoplennyh_rossiyskih_investitsiy_belarus__operezhaet_avstriyu_i_germaniyu____.html*.

199. Margarita Balmaceda, *Belarus: Oil, Gas, Transit Pipelines and Russian Foreign Energy Policy*, London, UK: GMB Publishing, 2006, p. 30.

200. European Union—EEAS (European External Action Service), Minsk, Belarus, available from *eeas.europa.eu/belarus/*.

201. "Yanukovich Podpisal Otkaz Ot NATO" ("Yanukovich Signed Refusal To Join NATO"), *24UA* July 15, 2013, available from *ru.tsn.ua/ukrayina/yanukovich-podpisal-otkaz-ukrainy-ot-nato.html*.

202. "Karasev: Ukrainsko-Rossiiskie Otnosheniya Zavisli v Neopredelennosti" (Karaves: The Ukrainian-Russian Relations Are At A Limbo), Ukrinfo News Agency, July 18, 2013, available from *www.ukrinform.ua/rus/news/ukrainsko_rossiyskie_otnosheniya_zavisli_v_neopredelennosti___karasev_1538605*.

203. Ronald Grigor Suni, *The Making of the Georgian Nation*, Bloomington, IN: Indiana University Press, 1994.

204. Jeffrey T. Checkel, "International Institutions and Socialization in Europe: Introduction and Framework," *International Organization*, Vol. 59, No. 4, International Institutions and Socialization in Europe, 2005, p. 805.

205. "Грузия Может Вступить В Евразийский Союз" ("Georgia May Join the Eurasian Union"), *PolitRUS*, June 13, 2013, available from *www.politrus.com/2013/06/13/georgia-russia-9/*.

206. The term borrowed from Andrew Wilson at the Kyiv Security Forum, Kyiv, Ukraine, April 2013.

207. Alexei Pikulik, "Prerequisites for Democracy, or Did Belarus Ever Have a Chance?" *Belarusian Institute of Strategic Studies*, October 22, 2012, available from *www.belinstitute.eu/en/node/409*.

208. The analysis is based on the public opinion poll, BISS 2010, "Social Situation in Belarus in 2009," conducted by Minsk, Balarus: The Research Center of the Institute for Privatization and Management.

209. Vital Silitski, "From Social Contract to Social Dialogue: Some Observations on the Nature and Dynamics of Social Contracting in Modern Belarus," Kiryl Haiduk, Elena Rakova, Vital Silitski, eds., *Social Contracts in Contemporary Belarus*, Minsk, Belarus: Belarusian Institute for Strategic Studies, p. 158.

210. James G. March and Johan P. Olsen, "The Institutional Dynamics of International Political Orders," *International Organization*, Vol. 52, 1998, pp. 943–969.

211. Steven Levitsky and Lucan Way, "The Rise of Competitive Authoritarianism," *Journal of Democracy*, Vol. 13, No. 2, April 2002, p. 52.

212. Larry Diamond, "Thinking about Hybrid Regimes," *Journal of Democracy* 13, No. 2, April 2002, p. 22.

213. A great example of this allowing a somewhat lackadaisical attitude to the signs of democratization in Georgia was the cartoon series, "Dardubala" (translated as a "disaster"), produced by an opposition channel and openly broadcast via public TV. In this show, then President Shevardnadze was depicted in a satirically negative way, together with the known (and mostly corrupt) local Georgian officials.

214. Philipp Krause, "Of Institutions and Butterflies: Is Isomorphism in Developing Countries Necessarily a Bad Thing?" *Background Note, The Overseas Development Institute*, April 2013, p. 1.

215. Thomas N. Sherratt, "The Evolution of Imperfect Mimicry," *Behavioral Ecology*, Vol. 13, No. 6, 2002, p. 821.

216. Paul J. DiMaggio and Walter W. Powell, "The Iron Cage Revisited: Institutional Isomorphism and Collective Rationality in Organizational Fields," *American Sociological Review*, Vol. 28, No. 2, 1983, p. 148.

217. Krause, p. 1.

218. Lant Pritchett, Michael Woolcock, and Matt Andrews, "Capability Traps? The Mechanisms of Persistent Implementation Failure," Working paper 234, Washington, DC: Center for Global Development, December 2010, p. 2.

219. DiMaggio and Powell, p. 150.

220. Frank Schimmelfennig and Ulrich Sedelmeier, eds., *The Europeanization of Central and Eastern Europe*, Ithaca, NY, and London, UK: Cornell University Press, 2005, p. 10.

221. Ben Rosamond, "Neofunctionalism," *Theories of European Integration*, Houndsmills, Basingstoke, UK: Palgrave Macmillan, 2000, pp. 50-73.

222. Checkel, p. 815.

223. Krause, p. 2.

224. Peter Evans, "Development as Institutional Change: The Pitfalls of Monocropping and the Potentials of Deliberation," *Studies in Comparative International Development*, Vol. 38, No. 4, Winter 2004, p. 33.

225. Marcin Święcicki, "Ukrainian Economy and Economic Reforms," Taras Kuzio and Daniel Hamiton, *Open Ukraine: Changing Course Towards a European Future*, Washington, DC: Johns Hopkins University Center for Transatlantic Relations, 2011, p. 65.

226. *Lessons from the Ukrainian Transition: Reform Driving Forces in a Captured State*, Warsaw, Poland: Center for Social and Economic Research, 2005, p. 1.

227. Alexander Kupatadze, "Ending Georgian Corruption Needs Institutional Reform," *Oxford Analytica*, January 2013.

228. Jim Nichol, "Georgia's October 2012 Legislative Election: Outcome and Implications," *Library of Congress*, Washington, DC: Congressional Research Service, October 15, 2012, p. 4.

229. "Georgian Parliament Adopts Sweeping Amnesty," *Radio Free Europe – Radio Liberty*, December 22, 2012.

230. Closing Press Conference by NATO Secretary General Anders Fogh Rasmussen following the meetings of NATO Defense Ministers, Brussels, Belgium, 2013, available from *www.nato.int/cps/en/natolive/opinions_101215.htm*.

231. European Union – EEAS.

232. Articles 1, 2, and 3 of the Constitution of Belarus, Minsk, Belarus, 1996.

233. "Лукашенко: "Российские Негодяи" Обвалили Калийный Рынок" ("Lukashenka: 'Russian Scoundrels' Crushed the Potassium Market"), Regnum, September 10, 2013, available from *www.regnum.ru/news/1705815.html*.

234. "Минск Меняет Москву на Пекин" ("Minsk Dumps Moscow For Beijing"), *GazetaRU*, July 17, 2013, available from *www.gazeta.ru/politics/2013/07/17_a_5433737.shtml*.

235. Bo Rothstein and Jan Teorell, "What Is Quality of Government? A Theory of Impartial Government Institutions," *Governance: An International Journal of Policy, Administration, and Institutions*, Vol. 21, No. 2, April 2008, p. 169.

236. Abraham H. Maslow, "A Theory of Human Motivation," *Psychological Review*, Vol. 50, 1943, pp. 370–396.

237. "Уровень Безработицы в Украине Снизился до 1.6%" ("Unemployment Level in Ukraine Down to 1.6%"), *UNIAN*, August 16, 2013, available from *economics.unian.net/rus/news/174639-uroven-bezrabotitsyi-v-ukraine-snizilsya-do-16.html*.

238. Steven Woehrel, "Ukraine: Current Issues and U.S. Policy," May 24, 2013, *Congressional Research Service*, 7-5700, RL33460, p. 6.

239. "Иванишвили Заявил о Неадекватных Действиях Властей Грузии в Августе 2008 Года" ("Ivanishvili Declared About Inadequate Actions of the Georgian Leadership in August 2008"), Russia-Georgia: Information Parity project, *News Georgia*, April 10, 2013, available from *georusparitet.com/official_statement/20130410/151555105.html*.

240. "The Hopes of Ivanishvili Regarding Russia," *The Messenger Online*, October 11, 2012, available from *www.messenger.com.ge/issues/2712_october_11_2012/2712_edit.html*.

241. "Иванишвили Еще Раз Подтвердил Намерение Уйти из Политики до Нового Года"("Ivanishvili Once More Confirmed His Desire To Leave Politics Before the New Year"), Georgia Online News Agency, August 23, 2013, available from *www.apsny.ge/2013/pol/1377319338.php*.

242. "Единственная Гарантия—Полный Отказ От ПРО" ("Complete Halt to the Antimissile Defense: The Only Guarantee"), *GazetaRU*, May 2, 2012, available from *www.gazeta.ru/politics/2012/05/02_a_4569905.shtml*.

243. "Рогозин про Системы ПРО: Выломает Всю Стену Если Нас Кто-то Попытается Изолировать" ("Rogozin's Take on Antimissile Defense: We will Crush the Whole Wall if Isolated"), *GazetaRU*, June 29, 2012, available from *www.gazeta.ru/politics/news/2012/06/29/n_2414157.shtml*.

244. National Statistics Office of Georgia, "Employment and Unemployment," *GeoStat*, available from *www.geostat.ge/?action=page&p_id=146&lang=eng*.

245. By an anecdotal coincidence, Bakradze is an alumnus of the Georgian Institute of Public Affairs (GIPA'96), whose rector was Margvelashvili in 2000–06 and in 2010–12.

246. "Участники Опроса Считают, Что Опасность Со Стороны России Преувеличена" ("The Respondents Think That the Threat from Russia Is Overestimated"), *News Georgia*, Russia-Georgia: Information Parity project, April 15, 2013.

247. "Зарегистрированная безработица в Беларуси сохраняется на уровне 0.6%" ("Registered Unemployment Level in Belarus Stays at a Level of 0.6%"), *BeltaNews*, April 9, 2013, available from *www.belta.by/ru/all_news/society/Zaregistrirovannaja-bezrabotitsa-v-Belarusi-soxranjaetsja-na-urovne-06_i_630389.html*.

248. Vital Silitski, "From Social Contract to Social Dialogue: Some Observations on the Nature and Dynamics of Social Contracting in Modern Belarus," Kiryl Haiduk, Elena Rakova, Vital Silitski, eds., *Social Contracts in Contemporary Belarus*, Minsk, Belarus: Belarusian Institute for Strategic Studies, p. 160.

249. Mark Kramer, "Ukraine, Russia, and U.S. Policy," *PONARS Policy Memo 191*, April 2001.

250. Volodymyr Dubovyk, "U.S.-Ukraine Relations: The Long Road to Strategic Partnership," *PONARS Policy Memo No. 424*, December 2006, p. 2.

251. U.S. Participation in the Kyiv Summit and the Chornobyl Pledging Conference: Fact Sheet, April 19, 2011, available from the State Department website, *www.state.gov/r/pa/prs/ps/2011/04/161228.htm*.

252. "Fact Sheet on Ukraine's Non-Proliferation Efforts," *Foreign Policy*, March 4, 2010.

253. Press release from the White House website, February 11, 2010, available from *www.whitehouse.gov/the-press-office/readout-presidents-call-with-president-elect-yanukovych-ukraine*.

254. Steven Woehrel, "Ukraine: Current Issues and U.S. Policy," May 24, 2013, *Congressional Research Service*, 7-5700, RL33460, Washington, DC: Congressional Research Service, p. 6.

255. "Urging the Government of Ukraine to ensure free and fair parliamentary elections on October 28, 2012, by adhering to democratic standards, establishing a transparent electoral process and releasing opposition leaders sentenced on politically motivated grounds," Washington, DC: U.S. Congress Resolution H. RES. 730, July 13, 2012.

256. U.S Department of State Statement on Parliamentary Elections in Ukraine, October 29, 2012, Washington, DC, available from *ukraine.usembassy.gov/statements/elections-ukraine-2012.html*.

257. Interview with Gunther Oettinger, the EU Commissioner for Energy, Kyiv, Ukraine, June 13-14, 2013, available from *ec.europa.eu/energy/international/bilateral_cooperation/ukraine_en.htm*.

258. Arkadiy Moshes, "Последний Довод" ("Last Reason") *Daily Journal*, August 22, 2013, available from *www.ej.ru/?a=note&id=13213*.

259. Leonid I. Polyakov, *U.S.-Ukraine Military Relations and the Value of Interoperability*, Carlisle, PA: Strategic Studies Institute, U.S. Army War College, 2004, p. 65.

260. Steven A. Carney, "Allied Participation in Operation 'Iraqi Freedom'," Washington, DC: U.S. Army Center of Military History, 2011, p. 116.

261. Website of the Ministry of Defense of Ukraine, available from *www.mil.gov.ua/index.php?part=peacekeeping&lang=en*.

262. "Armed Forces of Ukraine," *White Book 2011*, Kyiv, Ukraine: Ministry of Defense of Ukraine, 2012, p. 34.

263. Steven Woehrel, "Ukraine: Current Issues and U.S. Policy," *Congressional Research Service*, Washington, DC: Congressional Research Service, May 24, 2013, "Summary" section.

264. Polyakov, p. 65.

265. "United States-Ukraine Charter on Strategic Partnership," Washington, DC: U.S. Department of State, Bureau of European and Eurasian Affairs, available from *www.state.gov/p/eur/rls/or/142231.htm*.

266. U.S. Embassy in Ukraine *ukraine.usembassy.gov/odc.html*.

267. Russian Federation Foreign Policy Concept, adopted on February 12, 2013.

268. Andrey Mikhailov, "Is Ukraine ashamed of its infamous military cooperation with Georgia?" *Pravda.RU*, October 2, 2012, available from *english.pravda.ru/world/ussr/02-10-2012/122326-ukraine_georgia_military-0/*.

269. Zbigniew Brzezinski, "Russia, like Ukraine, will become a real democracy," *Financial Times*, December 10, 2013.

270. Goldstone, p. 286.

271. "Ivanishvili: We Will Get NATO MAP in 2014," *Eurasianet*, May 2, 2013, available from *www.eurasianet.org/node/66914*.

272. "Медведев: Вступление в НАТО Ничего Не Добавит Грузии" ("Medvedev: Membership of Georgia In NATO Will Bring No Benefits To Georgia"), *GazetaRU*, June 8, 2013, available from *www.gazeta.ru/politics/news/2013/08/06/n_3093897.shtml* .

273. "Allied Participation in Operation 'Iraqi Freedom'," p. 62.

274. "International Security Assistance Force, ISAF, Key Facts and Figures," October 1, 2013.

275. John Diedrich, "US faces tough training mission in the Caucasus," *The Christian Science Monitor*, May 30, 2002.

276. Jim Garamone, "U.S. Troops in Georgia to Begin Counterterrorism Training," American Forces Press Service, Washington, DC: U.S. Department of Defense, April 30, 2002, available from *www.defense.gov/News/NewsArticle.aspx?ID=44111*.

277. "Striking the Balance: U.S. Policy and Stability in Georgia," A Report to the Committee on Foreign Relations, Washington, DC: United States Senate, December 22, 2009, p. 5.

278. *Ibid.*, p. 6.

279. "International Military Education and Training Account Summary," Washington, DC: U.S. Department of State, June 23, 2010, available from *www.state.gov/t/pm/ppa/sat/c14562.htm*.

280. Irakli G. Areshidze, "Helping Georgia?" *Perspective*, Vol. 12, No. 4, March-April 2002, p. 3.

281. Tony Karon, "Why U.S. Arrival in Georgia Has Moscow Hopping Mad," *The Time*, February 27, 2002.

282. "Putin: Rossiya Nikogda Ne Sobiralas' Uxodit' Iz Zakavkaz'ya"("Putin: Russia Is Never Going To Leave Transcaucasus"), *GazetaRU*, December 2, 2013, available from *www.gazeta.ru/politics/news/2013/12/02/n_5787465.shtml*.

283. "Striking the Balance: U.S. Policy and Stability in Georgia," A Report to the Committee on Foreign Relations, Washington, DC: United States Senate, December 22, 2009, p. 5.

284. "United States-Georgia Charter on Strategic Partnership," Washington, DC: U.S. Department of State, Bureau of European and Eurasian Affairs, January 9, 2009.

285. Jack A. Goldstone, "Pathways to State Failure," *Conflict Management and Peace Science*, Vol. 25, 2008, p. 286.

286. Grzegorz Gromadzki, Vitali Silitski, and Luboš Veselý, "Effective Policy towards Belarus. A Challenge for the Enlarged EU," *European Choice for Belarus*, Warsaw, Poland: Stefan Batory Foundation/Association for International Affairs, April 2005.

287. Many of the nonprofit civil society organizations have moved to the neighboring countries, as the Belarusian Institute for Strategic Studies.

288. U.S. Government Act, "To provide for the promotion of democracy, human rights, and rule of law in the Republic of Belarus and for the consolidation and strengthening of Belarus sovereignty and independence," Public Law 108-347, 108th Cong., Washington, DC: U.S. House of Representatives, October 20, 2004, available from *https://bulk.resource.org/gpo.gov/laws/108/publ347.108.txt*.

289. Stewart Parker, *The Last Soviet Republic*, 2nd Ed., ebook, Great Britain,Commissar Books, 2011, p. 169.

290. Steven Woehrel, *Belarus: Background and U.S. Policy Concerns*, *Congressional Research Service* 7-5700, RL32534,Washington, DC: Congressional Research Service, February 12, 2013.

291. *Ibid*, p. 9.

292. Zalmay Khalilzad, "A Strategy of 'Congagement' toward Pakistan," *The Washington Quarterly*, Vol. 35, No. 2, 2012, pp. 107-119.

293. "Voennie Bazi Rossii Na Nashei Zemle" ("Russian Military Bases On Our Soil"), *Svobodnie Novisti*, available from *old.sn-plus.com/!_old-site_!/arhive/jan07/2/str/1-05.htm*.

294. Natalia Makushina, "Comment: Why Belarus Needs Third Russian Military Base," *Deutsche Welle*, September 6, 2013, available from *www.dw.de/комментарий-зачем-беларуси-третья-военная-база-россии/a-16868264*.

295. Website of the Ministry of Defense of the Republic of Belarus, *www.mil.by/ru/military_policy/rb_nato/*.

296. "Military and Technical Cooperation between Belarus and China," *Belarus Security Blog*, October 18, 2013, available from *www.bsblog.info/military-and-technical-cooperation-between-belarus-and-china/*.

ANNEX 1

QUESTIONNAIRE

Democratization and Instability in Ukraine, Georgia, and Belarus

5 = very high/very good

4 = high/good

3 = middling or ambiguous

2 =low/bad

1 = very low/very bad

1. What is the country of your origin?

___ Georgia   ___ Ukraine   ___ Belarus

All the remaining questions are regarding your country of origin, regardless of your current country of residence and will use the following answer scale:

5 = very high/very good

4 = high/good

3 = middling or ambiguous

2 =low/bad

1 = very low/very bad

Please pick one answer to each question:

Citizenship, Law, and Rights

1. To what extent is the rule of law operative throughout the country?

2. How independent are the courts and the judiciary from the executive?

3. How much confidence do you have in the legal system to deliver fair and effective justice?

4. How has the situation regarding democracy and human rights improved in the last decade?

5. How effective and equal is the protection of the freedoms of movement, expression, association and assembly?

6. How would you evaluate the situation with the freedom of speech?

7. How secure is the freedom for all to practice their own religion, language or culture?

8. How free from harassment and intimidation are individuals and groups working to improve human rights?

9. How would you assess the situation with economic freedom?

10. How satisfied are you with the economic development of your country?

Representative and Accountable Government

Did the elections become more transparent in the last decade?

___ Yes   ___ No

11. How free are opposition or non-governing parties to organize?

12. How much are you satisfied with the last elections held?

13. How much do you trust your government?

14. How comprehensive and effective is legislation giving citizens the right of access to government information?

15. How publicly accountable are the police and security services for their activities?

16. What is, in your opinion, the crime level in your country?

17. Do businesses influence public policy?

___ Yes   ___ No

18. How much confidence do you have that public officials and public services are free from corruption?

Civil Society and Popular Participation

19. How independent are the media from government?

20. How effective are the media and other independent bodies in investigating government and powerful corporations?

21. How free are journalists from restrictive laws, harassment and intimidation?

22. How independent are voluntary associations, citizen groups, social movements etc., from the government?

23. How much, in your opinion, is the influence of other countries on the domestic political affairs of your country?

24. Would you anticipate any significant political change in your country within the next 5 years?

____ Yes   ____ No

25. If you were to choose between economic stability and political freedom, which one would you prefer?

____ Economic stability   ____ Political freedom